Copyright & Disclaimers

The publisher and the author advise you to take full responsibility for your safety and know your limits. Before practicing the skills described in this book, be sure that your equipment is well maintained and do not take risks beyond your level of experience, aptitude, training, and comfort level.

The information and/or documents contained in this book do not constitute legal or financial advice and should never be used without first consulting with a financial professional to determine what may be best for your individual needs.

You should never make any investment decision without first consulting with your own financial advisor and conducting your own research and due diligence. To the maximum extent permitted by law, the publisher and the author disclaim any and all liability in the event any information, commentary, analysis, opinions, advice and/or recommendations contained in this book prove to be inaccurate, incomplete or unreliable, or result in any investment or other losses.

Content contained or made available through this book is not intended to and does not constitute legal advice or investment advice and no attorney-client relationship is formed. The publisher and the author are providing this book and its contents on an "as is" basis. Your use of the information in this book is at your own risk.

Dedications

To my amazing readers: I love you. I get you. I dedicate this to you so you can join me on my life journey and learn how to create the most extraordinary life for yourself. It's worth every single courageous second.

To Mom: For being the strongest woman, giving your whole entire world to me, and loving me more than humanly possible.

To Papa: For raising me to be a badass, independent, entrepreneur. Just like my papa.

To my dad: For teaching me the value of hard work and being just 5% better than anyone else.

To Ethan: For all of the love you show me and for being even better than the little brother I had always wanted growing up. This is just a tribute.

To Levi: For being my person. For being a man better than I could have imagined. For loving me extremely well, always. For being extraordinary. I love you so much. Forever.

To Aubrey: For reminding me that I deserve nothing less than the best since day 1.

To Kaitlyn: For being the #1 adventure buddy of all time.

To Kim Job: For taking a chance on a 23-year-old traveling nanny for her dream job.

To Brooke Castillo: For changing my whole entire life. All of it.

To my future children and grandchildren: Now you have some of my favorite stories from my first 27 years in one place (and maybe a little TMI), I can't wait to see what you create in the world. I love you.

Just For You

Throughout this book, I've created different exercises and questions for you to go through to help you create your extraordinary life. You can read this book along with a pen and paper to answer the questions, or you can download a PDF or Google Doc with all of the questions in one place for you at **createtheimpossiblelife.com/justforyou.**

Table of Contents

Introduction

I'm a big goal girl.

As soon as I learned how important having goals was to creating the life I wanted, I was all in. I like to think of goals like the ultimate life GPS. They guide us so we can get to any destination we want, no matter how far away it is. Without goals as our GPS, we would just drive around aimlessly for our whole life. Sometimes we might end up somewhere pretty cool. Other times we would end up somewhere and have no idea how we got there. Without a GPS or any guidance, we just kind of end up wandering around life, letting it take us wherever it takes us.

I didn't want an aimless life. I wanted an extraordinary life. I saw other women who had it all and they inspired me. I knew I could have it all too: a job or business I loved, working part-time, making the amount of money I wanted, an incredible romantic relationship and family, free time to get an iced coffee and go for a walk in the middle of the day, and just feeling happy.

I started learning everything I could. I read all of the books and took all of the courses. I found information that really helped me out and I applied it to my life. I hired incredible coaches and learned how to coach others. I started a business. I worked for people who were doing what I wanted to do in the world. And I changed my life completely.

One of my favorite things that I learned was how to set impossible goals. I had never heard of that before. In fact, I had usually heard of people setting small, attainable goals. "Realistic" goals. So that's what I had always done.

When I started setting impossible goals, my life started changing in HUGE ways, ways that truly blew my own mind. I went from making $40k to over $100k within 12 months. I went from hating running to running 12 half marathons and one full marathon within a year. I went from hating my body and having a disordered relationship with food to loving my body and having a healthy relationship with food. I went from genuinely thinking I'd be alone forever to being in the best relationship I could have imagined. OH... and I wrote a freaking book!

Impossible goals changed my life and so did all of the tools I've applied to my life that I'm about to share. I hope you enjoy the wild stories from every area of my life and apply what I've learned on my journey so you can create your own impossible life and achieve the extraordinary goals you've always wanted.

In this book, I'm going to share my failures and successes and everything I learned from them that helped me grow and become a confident, successful, grounded, loving human. Come on this journey with me and then let's go do some amazing things in this world.

Chapter 1: Why Create an Extraordinary Life

"If you're serious about changing your life, you'll find a way. If you're not, you'll find an excuse." —Jen Sincero

I was living a great life. I lived close to the beach. I had a family and awesome friends who loved me. I had a job and was making money. I was beautiful and healthy. I really did have it all. But it sure as hell didn't feel like it.

I had goals I wanted to achieve. I wanted to lose weight and get that tight, toned body of my dreams. I wanted to make at least $100k (but then I truly wanted to make millions one day doing something I loved and that made an impact on the world.) I wanted to be in a relationship with someone amazing, but I gave up on dating easily and was sure I had inherited the family curse of being forever alone. I wanted to travel the world, but also to stop stressing out about money. I wanted more free time because I felt like I was constantly busy and never had enough time to do all of the things I wanted to do. I wanted to go all-in on my own business, but I couldn't seem to give up the comfort and security of working for someone else. I wanted to just freaking love myself, to stop looking in the mirror and criticizing not just my body, but the person who I was.

I had it all. But I still felt like shit. I had a great life. But I wanted it to be extraordinary. I knew there was more for me.

If you're anything like I was, I want to help you create the life you truly deserve. Not because I have 100% of life figured out. I don't, and I don't think I ever will. But I've learned a damn lot on my journey, and I think the life I created is absolutely extraordinary. And I need to share everything I know with you.

The 80/20 of Life

"Trying to avoid sadness is trying to avoid life." —Maxime Lagacé

It was one of those days when allll of the super big, life-changing events that I had wanted for so long suddenly happened. I got a promotion at work AND I signed the papers to officially buy my first house. It should have been a super exciting day... but it wasn't. At all.

I actually was just sad. I made plans to go on a dinner date that night to celebrate. But the guy I was supposed to go with just stopped replying. Nothing. I asked my mom if we could go to dinner. She didn't want to. I asked my cousin. She had plans.

I expected this day to make me feel good, but I didn't feel good at all. I was so desperately trying to feel better. I just wanted to feel all of the exciting emotions I thought I would have felt.

I'm going to start off on an honest note. There's bad news in this book. Creating an extraordinary life can feel a lot like ass sometimes.

Doing this is going to involve a lot of feelings you'd really rather eat half a cake than feel. It's going to involve you getting uncomfortable a whole lot. It's going to involve failure like you've never failed before. It's going to involve shitty feelings when you think you should be feeling wonderful. And it's also going to be amazing.

Because once you understand and accept that the point of being a human is not to feel happy all of the time, you can lean into every part of your human experience and keep kicking ass even when you feel like ass. You get to create the life that you truly want. A life that you know you can create any result in. A life that is absolutely extraordinary and even beyond your wildest dreams.

I call this the 80/20 of life. (Or 70/30 or 50/50). The numbers aren't what are important. Knowing that life isn't supposed to be happy all of the time is what matters. Some of life feels pretty shitty. And the other part feels amazing. This is the human experience the way it was designed to be. (And if your life doesn't feel like it includes negative emotion, it's probably because you're using all kinds of things to distract yourself from feeling the more uncomfortable part.)

Let me walk you through the first half of my day today to explain how my 80/20 showed up for me. I woke up in a **super annoyed** mood. Why? I'm honestly not sure. I think I had a bad dream and felt some type of way about that. Then my boyfriend got up and was unusually chipper. He was being super bubbly and sweet and it made me **happy**. He got all of the pre—gym supplements out for me and grabbed me a towel to bring to the gym (because I forget to bring one more than half the time.) I was still **happy** and feeling **grateful**. We realized our normal trainer at the gym was out today so we'd have a sub. **Bummed**. Then we checked the schedule and realized it was our favorite sub! We were **excited** it was him. When I got to the gym, I felt **loved** saying hi to all of my friends there before class started. And felt a little **dizzy and sick** towards the end of the workout because it so hot and humid and we were workin' hardddd. I checked my watch at the end of my workout and realized I had burned 500 active calories during my workout. Super **proud** of me.

Some parts of my morning were great, and others didn't feel good. I typically don't make it through an entire day feeling wonderful.

Humans are not rainbow and butterfly robots. Humans are designed to feel the full range of emotions. And that includes the 20% that we don't love to feel.

But here's what I want you to consider. I think we do want to feel the negative emotions, too. I think we do want to feel grief when someone we love dies. I think we do want to feel upset when we see someone whom we love dearly upset. I think we do want to feel angry when we hear about all of the injustice in the world. If we could wave a magic wand and get rid of all of our negative emotions, I don't think we'd even want to. It would take away so much of our human experience. It'd be weird to be happy all of the time. And then happy wouldn't even be that fun if that's all we felt. So we're going to learn how to make the negative emotions not suck so bad.

And here's a little secret. Once you learn exactly what to do with those negative emotions instead of eating them, drowning them in wine, or scrolling to numb them, it won't even feel like 20% of life is negative emotion. You will become a badass at handling your emotions and they won't even feel all that negative anymore.

Exercise: Finding the 80/20

List a few negative emotions you felt today.

1.

2.

3.

For each feeling, identify why that negative feeling was necessary, wanted, or helpful in some way. This might take you some time, but keep thinking until you can find a reason. You can even Google it for ideas and to help your mind open up to this possibility.

Examples: I felt lightheaded today and it was a warning to my body that I needed to slow down. I felt anxious today. It didn't feel helpful at all, but it is a biological response to the stress in my life. (I'm not talking about anxiety disorder here). I felt bummed today and it was a feeling I wanted because I didn't get to see someone I loved that day who I thought I was going to see. Feeling bummed was a feeling I wanted to feel in that moment to honor the love I have.

Goals are Tough But So Are You

"All who have accomplished great things have had a great aim, have fixed their gaze on a goal which was high, one which sometimes seemed impossible." —Orison Swett Marden

This is not a book to teach you how to be happy all of the time. It's even better. It's going to teach you how to be extraordinary.

"I'm just happy with where I'm at. I don't need goals." This is what my mom would tell me when I was in my big goal-getter phase and would hound her about what her goals were. I didn't understand it. Why would someone not want to improve? To do better? To change? Whenever she tells me her unpopular opinions, she always concludes with, "You'll understand when you get older." Well...I understand now.

Goals are freaking hard. Uncomfortable. Challenging. And it's a hell of a lot easier to just stay the same and keep doing what you've always done. In fact, your brain highly prefers it.

Our brain's main job is to keep us alive. Which in our current times, it's amazing at. Our brain is wired to be motivated by something called The Motivational Triad. This includes seeking pleasure, avoiding pain, and conserving energy. This used to mean eating berries and having sex to reproduce, avoiding getting eaten by a wild animal, and staying in your cave so you didn't die. Now it means eating ice cream and drinking wine, avoiding anything uncomfortable or new, and staying in bed and watching Netflix.

What used to keep us alive is now what's killing us. The way our brain is designed, it won't create an extraordinary life for ourselves naturally anymore. It instead is set up to keep us stuck, avoiding reaching new goals, and staying the same. It just wants to keep us safe in our little cave with all of the immediate pleasures we crave.

We have to train our brain to do the opposite in order to create the extraordinary life we deserve. It's time to avoid false pleasures, take risks, invite discomfort, and put some effort in. Yes, even when it feels really hard.

So why should you create an extraordinary life when I already warned you it's not going to be all unicorns and lollipops? We set and accomplish goals for our own reasons. I don't know what your goals or reasons are specifically. You have to decide that for yourself. (And I suggest coming up with many very compelling reasons to reach your goals.)

Whys You Like

"When I read about the evils of drinking, I gave up reading."

—Henny Youngman

I used to drink alcohol. It's pretty normal. You've heard all of the sayings like "Alcohol. Because a good story never starts with a salad" or "Step aside coffee, this is a job for alcohol" or "Beer is the answer but I can't remember the question." Alcohol is a normal thing. People are questioned if they don't drink. Did you used to have a problem? Are you pregnant? It's as if the choice to not drink means something is wrong with you.

Have you ever thought about why you drink (if you do)? I thought about why I drank. It was so I wouldn't be questioned, so I could have more fun, and so it would be easier to talk to cute guys. What it really came down to was I didn't want to be the odd one out, the different one. Being the odd one out would make me the first person in the tribe to be thrown to the lions. Brains still work very similarly to how they used to.

The more I thought about why I drank, the clearer it became that it was for other people's approval and the more it started to bother me. I didn't like that reason. I didn't like why I drank.

I have a friend who stopped drinking and she recommended the book *This Naked Mind* by Annie Grace. From that book, I learned that the most harmful drug is alcohol. Not meth, heroine, cocaine, or LSD. It's alcohol. That totally took me by surprise. This gave me even more of a reason to go with what I had known about myself all along. I had found another why for quitting alcohol. Then I started dating the most wonderful man who didn't drink and we had so much fun not drinking together—another reason to not drink alcohol. I drank a few more times in social situations and continued to feel like absolute shit afterwards, which was yet again another reason to stop drinking.

The whys kept piling up. And one day I just simply made a decision. I wasn't a person who drank anymore. And I'm damn proud of it.

You need whys to go with every goal. Here are some of the reasons that I want to create an extraordinary life:
- Because it can be really fun to blow my own mind.
- To see what I'm fully capable of.
- To be an example of what is possible to everyone around me.

- To evolve myself as a human.
- Because life is going to be half shitty with or without my goal anyways. So I might as well create something amazing.

I'm going to guess this isn't the first time you've read or heard anything in the lovely self-help category, and therefore it's not the first time you've heard "make sure you have a why." Everyone tells you this because it is very important that you have a compelling reason for the changes you want to make. This is the "why" behind your goal. You need to have something to remember when shit hits the fan (because it will) and you just want to give up. The more compelling your why is, the more committed you will be to your goal.

And I'll be honest here, it is important to have reasons why we do what we do. But you need to LIKE your why. Make sure the reason you're doing what you're doing is a reason you like. Your reason should motivate you. You should even have multiple whys because sometimes one reason just isn't going to be enough when times get hard. Your why has to carry you through all of the discomfort and obstacles and struggle. It should be such a strong why that none of the doubt matters. The emotion of your why needs to be stronger than your doubt. It needs to keep you going when you're tired, frustrated, and confused. If not, you won't keep going.

Here's what I mean.
Here are some "whys" that probably aren't going to work well:
- So that a person in my life will be happy or like me more.
- Because I won't hate myself anymore when I do it.
- To feel like a worthy human.

You don't have enough power to control other people's happiness. Achieving a goal isn't what makes you love yourself—that's a whole different story. And you're 100% worthy as you are. I'm not saying you shouldn't want people to be happy or you shouldn't do things to hate yourself less or that you shouldn't feel more worthy. That's not it at all.

I say these whys aren't going to work because they are inside jobs. They can only be accomplished from the inside out; a goal isn't going to get you there. They are things we all want and try to achieve through external events like goals. But what we really need to work on is our minds. Start going to therapy (I just started too), get a coach, read personal development books and listen to educational podcasts, journal, get a mentor, take more time alone without distractions, and learn (things they typically don't teach in school.)

Your goals are not what make you a worthy human. They aren't guaranteed to make other people love you more. And accomplishing a goal isn't going to make you love yourself. That's the work you have to do outside of the big goals I'm talking about here.

Oh, and in the process of accomplishing goals, I also absolutely do think that in my own experience I have learned to love myself more and have grown tremendously as a person. I just don't want the intention of accomplishing a goal to be any of those reasons because that's not a goal's job. It's yours.

OK, now that we have that out of the way, here are some whys that I think are super helpful:

- To become a person doing things that change the world.
- To earn more money to do good.
- To become closer to the version of myself I want to be.
- To inspire the people around me and show them that yes, I can be an amazing parent and business owner AND have a hot bod. And not be too busy at all.
- To advocate for people or things that can't advocate for themselves.
- To look even more amazing in a bikini.
- Because I want to and it feels good, exciting, or fun.

You can choose any of these whys or any of your own. Just make sure YOU like the reason behind why you want a particular goal. Your why should keep you going through all of the obstacles that will come up between you and your dreams.

My Whys

"Find your why and you'll find your way." —John C. Maxwell

These are the whys I personally really like and use at the moment for myself. I've been so inspired by learning about other women's whys, so I want to share my own with you. If they resonate with you, you can use them in your own life or use them as inspiration to create your own incredible whys.

My Why #1: I think it's really fun to achieve things I never thought I was capable of.

I was never a runner. I never liked running. I was the kid that had to lie about my mile time in middle school so that I wouldn't fail PE. I thought people who ran for fun might have something wrong with them, until one day I found out I was one of those insane people myself.

Every inch of my body was covered in sweat. I couldn't even feel very much anymore. But I did know I was still sore from a hike I did a couple of days ago. I looked up to see palm trees and a breathtaking view of the ocean. One mile to go. That's it. I can do this.

I was in Honolulu, Hawaii. I took the trip completely alone to run my first (and probably last) full marathon: 26.2 miles. If I was going to run a damn marathon, I was going to Hawaii to do it.

I ran the entire thing without stopping. And as I neared the finish line, I heard a group of the new friends I had met at the hostel that week yelling my name. My heart was completely full. My legs were completely toast. And I had just completed a full f-ing marathon.

In 2019, I set a goal. A crazy goal. A goal I only set because it seemed like a super fun way to blow my own mind and see what I was capable of. The goal was to run 12 half marathons in 12 different states during 2019. I figured it was a good excuse to travel all year and a great way to get an amazing body. About halfway through the year, I realized (and hoped) I might never run as much as I currently was ever again, and if I was ever going to run a full marathon, this would be the time to do it.

The year wasn't easy. It was filled with many tears and physical therapy appointments. But I freaking did it. I ran 12 half marathons and one full marathon in 12 different states in 2019. Florida. Louisiana. Washington. California. Virginia. Illinois. Arizona. Georgia. New York. Texas. Nevada. Hawaii. Just for fun. Just because I thought it would be something kind of crazy I could do. Something I never thought I could have done. Something I would remember for a lifetime. And I will remember it forever. I ran 26.2 miles in Hawaii, because I thought accomplishing it would show me what I was capable of and blow my mind. It did.

 It was exciting. I was in awe of myself. It was kind of like the first time I ran seven miles straight. I was in complete awe that my body and mind could do that. I typically really, really want to stop running within about the first 20 seconds, so finishing seven miles felt unreal. I was so impressed with myself. That feeling just kept increasing. I was capable of so much more than I thought. I was in awe. I was excited. That's what kept me going. The awe and excitement drove me to keep taking actions towards my goal. They kept me motivated when everything hurt and I felt like I was dying. I love using this why. I think it's really fun to achieve things I never thought I was capable of. It keeps me going, it keeps me having fun, and it keeps me on a path of creating an extraordinary life.

My Why #2: I want to see what I'm fully capable of.

I was living in Melbourne, Australia in 2018 and I was about to start working on Life Coach Certification and I had just set my very first impossible goal. It was a Saturday afternoon in January and I had got back to the apartment after a long morning out, still in my sweaty gym clothes. I immediately collapsed face down on the bed crying. "Why am I like this?" "Why do I have to set such huge, crazy goals?" "Why can't I just be normal like everyone else?" (Since I'm being honest here, I still have those thoughts sometimes even now...brains love safety and security, which aren't guaranteed with huge goals in the picture.) My boyfriend at the time, Ryan, and all of his friends were at the apartment drinking and playing games.

I had just come home from a Lululemon goal—setting event. I'm not usually the person to speak up in a group setting, but I wanted to challenge myself to get out of my comfort zone at this event. "My goal for this year is to make $100k," I told the entire group. I instantly felt like I needed to justify that I wanted to help people, and that I'd use the money for "good" things. I didn't want them to think I was greedy. And who was I anyway to be making so much money?

I went to school for freaking Child Development. My highest paying job up to this point provided me $25 per hour (which felt like a damn lot) and I only could get part-time hours. Just saying that I wanted to make $100k out loud created negative thoughts about myself and uncomfortable, unworthy feelings. Plus I had no idea how I was going to make it happen. The most I had ever made in a year was a little under $40k.

And then something incredible happened. I made $114k that year. (You'll find out more about how later. I didn't become a stripper.)

Reaching this goal felt incredible. It was unreal and so fun. I set the goal at that event and then by the end of the year I proved to myself that I was capable of so much more than I had ever thought. Achieving this helped me see that my future was going to be better than I had even imagined. When I'm 80 years old, I want to look back and not regret anything I didn't do or try. I want to look back and know that I gave this one life my all. By setting a goal that felt impossible to me, I pushed myself to achieve something and I got to see what I was truly capable of. Learning that made me feel like I could truly accomplish anything I set my mind to.

My Why #3: I want to be an example of what is possible to everyone around me.

You've heard about Roger Bannister, right? He's the four-minute mile guy, the first man that ran a mile under four minutes. After he did it, thousands of other people did it too. It wasn't running a mile in under four minutes that was impossible. It was that we all THOUGHT it was impossible. There's a big difference there.

Once he was an example of what was possible to the world, thousands of other people also duplicated this incredible accomplishment. He just proved it could be done. I want to be a Roger Bannister to someone...to a lot of people. I want to be that example of doing extraordinary things so that other people will see me and say, "Well, if she can do it, then I can do it too."

You can do this too. HELL YEAH, YOU CAN. There's room for all of us in the extraordinary life club.

When I was traveling in Thailand, I got invited to a Digital Nomad Summit. This was a conference where all kinds of people who worked online and traveled the world got together. These people typically made regular U.S. salaries (in other words, higher than the rest of the world) but managed to have super low living expenses because they were nomads and worked wherever their travels took them across the globe. That weekend, I decided I would do whatever it took to become a digital nomad. I wanted to work AND travel. I wanted it all.

I started off as an au pair (live-in nanny) in New Zealand. Then I got a job working for my all-time favorite company doing remote customer support. Later I got promoted to the Director of Customer Support there and then Director of Marketing. I was making $150k with six weeks of paid time off. We even got paid to go to work meetings in places like the Cayman Islands. I got paid to go jet skiing on a Monday. I had my dream job AND I was traveling the world. I made my dream come true, and I wanted to show other people they could have it all, too.

I loved sharing my adventures on social media, and all of my friends were always eager to see where I went next. I had a travel blog where I shared how to travel on a budget so it could be accessible to more people. People started messaging me, asking how I was able to work and travel. My coworkers saw that I could do an amazing job at work and be in a beautiful place. They told me they were inspired to start traveling while working remotely, too.

I love sharing my story with everyone I come in contact with because I want more people to know that possibilities truly are endless. You don't have to work in a cubicle until you die. There are tons of people living their best life without ever stepping foot in a cubicle... and making a ton of money doing it. And I get to be an example to you, too. I need you to know there is more out there. You don't have to settle for a job you don't like. You can make more money. You can travel as much as you want to. And if you want, you can also be an example of the life that's possible to other people. It'll keep the goals you set and life you're creating pretty dang amazing, too.

My Why #4: I want to evolve myself as a human.

e·volve /ē'välv/ — to develop gradually, especially from a simple to a more complex form

I decided a long time ago that I didn't want to be normal. I didn't want a normal life. I didn't want to do what everyone else was doing. And I sure as hell didn't want to be that person who when asked, "So what's new?" says, "Nothing, really."

I want to be different. Fun. Exciting. I want to get the absolute most out of this one life I get. And to do that, I need to do the hard stuff — the stuff that pushes me, that changes me, that teaches me a lot, even when it feels crappy to learn the lesson.

So here I am writing a book and I'm 26-years-old.

I have SO much more to learn. And I have SO much more life to live. And I'm probably going to say or do the wrong things some of the time.

I'm not yet as much of an activist as I think I should be. I'm not vegan yet, even though I'm pretty sure that will really help this planet that I love so much. I'm still learning to do better as a human. I've only been with my current boyfriend for 10 days as I write this, so I can't really say I'm a relationship expert. Add all of this to the 500 other crappy thoughts I think about myself and it tells me that I shouldn't be writing this book.

But hi, here I am. I'm putting myself out there and doing some scary, vulnerable shit to evolve myself because it's worth going through that to become more of who I want to be.

My Why #5: Life is going to be half shitty with or without my goal anyways. I might as well create an amazing life.

I was sitting on the floor of a big, fancy upgraded room in Caesars Palace. Black tears were running down my face. I was sitting next to the window with a gorgeous view of Las Vegas. I could barely breathe because I was crying so hard.

I took a video of myself while I was crying because it was the most wild thing to me that my life was so good but I was still so sad.

It was the opening day of Las Vegas after COVID on June 4th, 2020, after COVID had shut down the whole world for months. I had a perfectly good, free, king bed to sleep in at my grandpa's house 30 minutes away. But I wanted to treat myself and be right in the heart of Vegas on reopening day. I wanted to go out and work by the pool. I wanted to go for walks at night and early in the morning. (Walking the Vegas strip early in the morning when no one else is there is my favorite thing.) I wanted to be closer to my favorite country bar in the whooole world so I could stay out a little later and have my bed a little closer. I was excited for a little getaway.

Life felt so damn hard that week. I was really, really sad. But I was in a fancy hotel while I was sad. It was during the time when Black Lives Matter riots were happening and both myself and the company I managed marketing for had a LOT to learn. There was a lot of shame happening all around.

My life looked amazing on Instagram. (I mean, as usual, whose doesn't, right?) But just because life appears amazing on the outside doesn't mean it feels amazing. I felt really shitty. But because I had accomplished my huge goal and was making good money, I had the privilege of feeling shitty in a fancy hotel.

Life is GOING to suck sometimes. It sucks to always eat healthy and it sucks to not have the body you want. It sucks to work all the time and it sucks to not have money. It sucks to be single and alone and it sucks to take on all of the new changes that come with a relationship. No matter which life path you choose, it's not going to be all sunshine and rainbows. Either way, life is part shitty and part amazing.

We get to make the choice. If you knew either path you took would have negative parts, which one would you want? I'd rather choose the hard one that comes with eating healthy than the hard that comes with an unhealthy body. I'd rather choose the hard that comes with furthering my career and business than the hard one that comes with money struggles and knowing I'm doing less than what I'm capable of. I'd rather choose the hard one that comes with a committed relationship than the hard one that comes with being single.

Life is going to be challenging no matter which path you choose. No matter how much money you make. No matter how smokin' hot your partner is. No matter how smart your first born is. No matter how defined your abs are. Life is going to be shitty sometimes. And honestly...if it's going to be shitty sometimes, I'd rather choose feeling shitty in a fancy hotel.

Knowing that any decisions you make will come with negative emotion, and you really, truly can't escape it by choosing what seems easier in the moment, what amazingness do you want to create?

Exercise: Your Whys

Answer these questions to find your compelling whys for what you want to accomplish.

1. What is the accomplishment you're most proud of in your life so far? Was it graduating college? Having a baby? Getting an award? Performing on a stage?

2. Once you've thought of the accomplishment you're most proud of, ask yourself all of the reasons why you did it. Your reasons might be something like: I knew it would make the rest of my life so much better, I wanted to prove to myself that I could do it, I wanted to change the world in a positive way, or I wanted to overcome my fear.

3. Would those reasons inspire you to accomplish other goals that feel huge, impossible, and kind of scary? If so, keep going. If not, go back and try to find reasons that might help you with accomplishing other goals, too.

4. How do you feel when you think about those whys? Do you feel motivated, excited, or compelled? If so, they might be great whys to use for other goals.

5. What other whys have you heard that have inspired you to be more of the person you want to be? Feel free to borrow those, too!

Overcoming Fear & Creating Massive Courage

"As the physically weak man can make himself strong by careful and patient training, so the man of weak thoughts can make them strong by exercising himself in right thinking." —James Allen

If you could wake up tomorrow with any trait just given to you, what would it be?

I always say the trait I would want is having a massive amount of courage. Having a lot of courage would absolutely change my life. Just imagine a typical day that didn't involve fear. Who would you talk to? What would you say? What would you wear? How would you show up differently? Now imagine an entire life without fear. What would you do every day? You might do things you really, truly want to do if you absolutely believed that there was nothing to be afraid of.

Imagine a life where you weren't scared of running out of money.
Imagine a life where you weren't scared of what others would think.
Imagine a life where you weren't scared of insecurity or instability.
Imagine a life where you weren't scared of massive failure.
Imagine a life where you weren't scared of disappointing yourself or your loved ones.

Here's the best news ever. Overcoming fear is possible. Massive amounts of courage are possible. Courage is something that we learn, and something you can get more of. But first it's important to know that fear is amazing and helpful. Fear kept us alive. Fear still keeps us alive. It keeps us from driving 150 mph. It keeps us away from the edge of a cliff (unless Instagram photos are involved and that's a different story). It keeps us alert so our children and puppies stay safe. Fear is helpful...until it's not.

Currently, fear is the main thing holding us back from creating an extraordinary life.

I woke up on a spring morning on a sticky leather couch. I was in Atlanta, Georgia. There was a messy pile of my clothes spilling out of my bag next to me. It took me a second to realize where I was. Oh, right. I was couchsurfing. You know, couchsurfing. It's kind of like Airbnb...well, except it's totally free...you hang out with the host (who is a complete stranger that you find on the internet), the house usually isn't very clean, and you're just sleeping on the couch in their living room.

I typically travel alone. The couchsurfing hosts are usually single men. I've couchsurfed a little over 10 times all across the world. Some experiences have been fine, and most have been so fun. Maybe it's courage, or if you're one of those crime podcast people, it's stupidity. Either way, I count it as overcoming fear. I believe 100% in my core that people are good. I trust my gut instinct 100% of the time. Trusting people too much is 100% my character flaw. And I 100% love a free place to sleep.

Couchsurfing is one of the many things I do that requires courage. I've been both skydiving and bungee jumping. But I also left my director-level remote position in the middle of a pandemic when unemployment rates were peaking to do what I truly wanted...with no guarantee of any money or success. I've traveled to many countries totally alone, including places like Mexico and Colombia. I've traveled around the United States in a van with just my puppy, Wilder. I've asked for a raise many times, including directly to the owner of the company I worked for. I've started a business. I used to sneak into all kinds of events and award shows in LA to meet celebrities (and damnnn was I good at it.)

I've taken pole dancing and twerking classes, just alone and not even with friends. I competed in a bikini bull riding competition at some bar, totally sober. (Just thinking about this one makes me feel super cringy. It was THAT uncomfortable for me. I'm not the girl to do that kind of thing...okay, well, apparently I am.) What requires tons of courage for me is probably different than what requires tons of courage for you. But it's SO important to learn the skill of overcoming fear in order to create the life you truly want.

It's crucial to be okay with fear being there and just doing the thing anyway. Fear is always going to be in your way. Always. It stops a damn lot of people. Please don't let it stop you. Just bring it with you in your back pocket and take over the world.

Exercise: Creating Courage

Here's my favorite exercise for creating massive amounts of courage: Dare yourself to do something different each day for 30 days straight. There should be different dares every single day. Each dare just has to be something that truly feels scary and uncomfortable. It's going to be different for everyone, but here are some ideas:

- Take a dance class
- Ask for an upgrade
- Take a trip alone
- Dance in your car while making eye contact with the stranger at the stoplight next to you
- Do an Instagram Live for at least five minutes
- Start a real conversation with a stranger
- Be the first one to say I love you
- Ask for a discount on your coffee without any reason for asking
- Take a stand up comedy class
- Go out to dinner alone

Write down your 30 dares. Then do them!

The more you practice feeling fear and doing it anyway, the easier it gets and the more you'll realize you won't die (even though it seriously feels like it sometimes.) You'll create that massive courage and confidence in yourself and you'll have the courage to create your extraordinary life.

The Struggle to Change

"I believe that God gives you hopes and dreams in a size that's too large, so you have something to grow into." —Lynn A. Robinson

Remember when I said creating your extraordinary life is going to feel like ass sometimes? When you have your current life, and want more and you're changing, it feels miserable. Expect it to.

Maybe in the beginning, it will feel good and exciting, but the longer we work towards our goal and the closer we get to reaching it, the more our minds will freak out. If we don't see ourselves as the person who has reached that goal yet (which we likely won't since we haven't reached that goal), our brain will convince us to go back to the person who we've always been. The person who we've always been has kept ourselves alive and done pretty well for our whole life, and it would be pretty safe to just keep doing that over and over and over forever. This will cause a ton of discomfort. That place between where you are now and where you want to be is one of the most uncomfortable spots to be in.

Nothing has gone wrong if you don't feel amazing all of the time. This means everything is working exactly how it's supposed to. Human brains love efficiency and doing what they've always done. Human brains hate change. Your brain will throw literally everything it can at you to get you to stop this cute little change thing. You're probably pretty smart. Which means your mind knows exactly how to convince you to get what it wants. It will feel conflicted. "Write your book, but people you love are going to be upset about it and the things you say in it." "Follow your meal plan, but you're going to be super annoying to everyone for wanting to eat something different." "Train for the marathon, but know if you do your knees are going to be screwed up for the rest of your life." "Reach your money goal but then it'll be really weird around your friends if you're making the most money." These are all thoughts that have gone through my mind at some point while I was in the process of achieving an impossible goal. They feel absolutely terrible. They're not even necessarily true, but my mind just came up with the best reasoning it could to get me to stop doing scary things. The animalistic part of your brain is begging you to stay the same and please just lay down and watch some tv. The evolved part of your brain is begging you for growth, purpose, and an extraordinary life. Recognize when your mind is making up stories and creating resistance to try to get you to stay where you're at. Don't give in to the animalistic brain. Keep going. Know that this transition time is going to suck. It's supposed to.

Exercise: What's Keeping You Stuck
When you're reaching for any big goal, your mind will do it's absolute best to keep you from massive change. It's doing its job to keep us safe. But we are safe. And we need to keep going.

1. Think of a goal you have not yet completed. What thoughts are holding you back? Are they true or just stories?

2. When those thoughts come up and they make you want to slow down or stop and how can you keep going anyways? (For example, listen to my favorite self—belief meditation, think about

the person or people I'd be helping by achieving my goal, go for a walk to re-center, etc.)

3. What would happen if that bad thing in your thoughts actually happened? What if they did get mad or annoyed at you for working towards your goal? Would you still do it?

Unshakable Belief

"Don't believe everything you think." —Byron Katie

I got my dream job at 25, but it wasn't an easy process. I totally had lost faith that getting that job was even possible for me. I only achieved it because I kept going. I had an unshakable belief when I had no evidence at all that things were going to go my way.

I'll start all the way at the beginning. I was hired as a part-time Customer Support Representative with the possibility of becoming full-time in the company soon. But it wasn't just any company. It was a company I was obsessed with. The owner of the company had changed my life and it was unreal to be able to work for her AND the job was 100% remote (which I was dying for) AND I would be making almost twice what I had made in any other job. It was a pinch-me-I'm-dreaming job. I was 23 at that point. I had never had a "real" job before. I had never worked full-time. I had never worked in a corporate environment or in an office. My job history included snack bars, restaurants, Domino's Pizza, multiple preschools, and all of the babysitting jobs. I liked flexible jobs where I could take a lot of time off to travel. I liked jobs where I could multitask, like babysitting, where I could get homework or blogging done at the same time. I never learned how to be professional or follow a strict work schedule. I wanted my life to be more important than my job and it was apparent in the way I showed up for work.

When I started the part-time job, I checked emails when it was convenient for me. I attended our team meetings with the owner of the company while I was at airports with loud people, announcements, and terrible wifi. I was completely ignorant to the fact that I was completely blowing it. I didn't know these were terrible ideas. I didn't know how important it was to show up professionally. I was just super excited to have an online, flexible job and I was happy to be there.

Thankfully, the company was amazing. They taught me instead of moving on to the next person. Fortunately they gave me another chance. I grew *a lot* in my position. I took initiative and helped out all of the other departments. People within the company then started coming to *me* for help.

The people all around me were constantly changing. The company had high standards. They created incredible results in the business and only hired the best of the best. Many people just didn't fit. There were only two other people still with the company when I left who were there when I started.

I trained people to be my manager, but I continued to stay in the same position. I watched the rest of the team go on amazing work trips together that I wasn't invited to. I listened to the owner tell everyone about how much she loved her full-time employees and then gave them each a $50k bonus for Christmas.

Honestly, it hurt. I was super bummed. I wanted it all so bad. I wanted to be officially on the team. I wanted to be full-time. I wanted to go on the trips and help make the decisions.

I considered quitting. I wondered if there was another company that would appreciate me more. One of the goals I put on my vision board for the year was to become a full-time employee, but by June I gave up on the idea all together. They didn't want me full-time. I was specifically told that. They needed amazing people to build the business, and I was less than amazing. I didn't blame them. I was young and I had a lot to learn.

But I kept going. I didn't let no mean no. I did everything in my power to keep growing and learning. I figured out exactly how a director would show up and I started doing that. I didn't give up no matter how much it felt like I wasn't making progress.

Two years. It took two years of me trying to get a full-time position and failing. I kept asking. I kept trying. I kept saying yes and doing more than I needed to. I kept doing everything in my power I could do.

But I just wasn't making the progress I wanted to make. I didn't know that it would ever change. It looked like I would never make the progress I wanted to make. And I decided to just keep going, no matter what the result was. I kept going when there was no evidence that it was working.

And then one day when I was working at the Hyatt by the ocean in my nice clothes (because the woman I wanted to be dressed up and worked in fancy places where she could feel amazing and stay focused), my manager, Kim, messaged me and asked if I could meet with her. Am I fired? I thought. I had no idea what this could be about. And when we got on the call, she asked me if I would accept the position of Director of Customer Support.

!!!

The dream job. Exactly what I wanted for so long. I had no idea it was coming.

Not only did it work out, but I then ended up getting promoted to the Director of Marketing. The CEO said it was the most important position on the team. I was very close to the top of the company and I was the employee that had been with the company the longest.

My consistent action to get there, even when it felt like I was making no progress, is what got me there. I chose to keep trying even when I had no reason to believe I was getting closer to my goal. Sometimes it's going to feel like you're not getting anywhere. Sometimes you might want to quit because the result you want isn't coming fast enough. It might feel like that for years. But what's the rush?

My success was due to one thing: an unshakable belief in myself. When they told me no, I didn't believe them. I kept going. I showed up as a top employee even though I was a part-time contractor. I believed that it would all be worth it. I believed I had so damn much potential and I made the decision that I would keep going even when it felt hard. I believed in myself when no one gave me any reason to. And then I showed up like the person I wanted to be. I kept that unshakable belief in myself and got myself into the job I wanted. The dream job. (And a few months later I got to play on a jetski on a Monday afternoon in the Cayman Islands...while getting paid.)

So, I want you to just commit to one thing while going through this book. Is it a money goal, a weight goal, a career goal, a relationship goal? Whatever it is for you right now, decide to believe in you, to believe it's possible, to believe no matter what, it's going to happen as long as you keep going. Believe it even when all signs point to the opposite. The dream is coming. Keep. Going.

Exercise: When You Want to Give Up

1. What do you truly want which you feel like you're not making progress towards?

2. Describe how you would feel if you had it now.

3. Why would you feel that way?

4. Notice you just created that feeling with your thoughts when you answered number two. Achieving that goal isn't what will make you feel better. Your mind is what will.

5. Why are you in a rush to achieve this goal?

6. Are you willing to keep going even when there is no evidence that you're making progress? Why or why not?

7. What advice would your 80-year-old self give you?

8. At what point will you want to decide to stop trying this and move on? How will you know to change directions?

9. What can you tell yourself when the doubt creeps in and you feel like you want to quit?

Moving Forward Without Knowing The How

"Take the first step in faith. You don't have to see the whole staircase, just take the first step." —Dr. Martin Luther King Jr.

"Ok, so what do I need to do?" I started laughing after I asked the question. "I swear, I ask you this every single week." I was on my weekly coaching call and asking the famous question I always want the answer to. Apparently, I'm not the only one who asks about this often. I always want to know how, what to do, and what steps I need to take next.

Once we decide that we want change, our mind immediately starts freaking out about how it's going to happen. We want to know what the correct next step is. Which diet should I follow? Which business should I start? What should I invest in? Where should I meet people to find amazing dates? And while all of this seems super important, it's not. Your unshakable belief is much more important, I promise.

Here's the thing. If I told you exactly the steps you needed to take to create the extraordinary life you want (the how), and then just one or two things didn't work, you would believe everything was ruined. If we have a specific, perfect plan laid out and we are set on it, the moment something doesn't work, we usually stop trying. We give up. We think that the plan didn't work and that now we can't get what we want. This is how I used to feel about a diet. If it didn't work (and work fast) I'd just give up. The plan was broken. Then I had an excuse to just stop trying and go back to the comfort I was used to.

I truly do wish I could give you a 100% guaranteed list of steps that would get you to your goal. Unfortunately, I can't give you that, but I can show you how to create your own plans. That's "plans," plural. There isn't one perfect plan. There are a hundred imperfect plans. And it can be either super fun or super exhausting to figure out your perfect plan. It's up to you to decide.

If you truly have an unshakable belief in yourself, and your first 99 plans fail, can you keep going? That's the big secret. You must be willing to fail, to massively fail and fall flat on your face and then keep going. And going. And going. And going.

Failure is discouraging, especially when we've been raised to avoid it at all costs. Failure sucks. It's hard and it feels terrible. It creates negative emotion and our human brain would prefer to just do things we already know we're good at. Say it with me: *If nothing changes, nothing changes.* What if you could learn to love failure?

The terrible part of failure is what we make it mean about ourselves. Answer the question, so what if you failed? Your answer might be something like: "This always happens to me. It's never going to work the way I want it to. I'm just not made for this. I can't do it. Nothing is working." Those thoughts feel terrible. They're definitely not fun or amazing or encouraging. They will likely lead to activities that will get you further from your goal. So how could you ever go from thoughts like that to loving failure?!

First, you have to fully experience failure on its own without all of the negative self—talk that has likely accompanied it every time you've failed in the past. Failing does not mean *anything* negative about you. It's just an event, and it doesn't mean you're not going to reach your goal. Experience the failure. What happened? It was hard. There were probably still some negative feelings, but you didn't die. You made it. It probably wasn't even as bad as you worried it would be. Can you be willing to put yourself through it again if you knew it would help you get closer to your goal? Practice feeling that discomfort.

Andy Frisella talks about "Test Days." They are the days that are super hard. The days you fail. The days you feel terrible. He talks about those days being the absolute most important ones because they are the ones that make us stronger. When we can learn to love and look forward to the days that are the most challenging, we will become unstoppable. And I love this concept because I think it's so true. Once we can learn to be okay with, and even like the difficult days and moments, we become so much stronger. We can handle hard emotions. We can grow because we've mastered our own mind.

Failure can be amazing because you can learn so much from it. Failure is ESSENTIAL to your success. The more you fail, the more you learn, the closer you are to your goal. The exact steps to get there aren't what's important.

The formula for success is this:
unshakable belief in yourself + failure + learning = success

The how isn't an essential part of the equation. Don't worry about it if you don't know how you're going to get where you want to go right now. You're not supposed to know, and that's supposed to feel super scary. Just find one step that might work. Then find another step that might work. It's not about knowing exactly what to do, it's about always moving forward. Failing. Failing again. Persistence. You'll find the how if you keep going, I promise.

That's Why

So that's why I think creating an extraordinary life is pretty damn awesome.

Because life is going to be 80/20 anyways and there are going to be negative parts whether you're creating something extraordinary or not.

Because you're tougher than you know, and setting huge goals is an amazing way to see your potential.

Because I have a whole list of other whys that keep me going when I don't want to, and after exploring this for yourself, hopefully you have some amazing ones, too.

Because an extraordinary life will help you overcome fear and create massive courage.

Because it'll help you create an unshakable belief in YOU.

And because you will be able to move forward and keep going even when it feels like you don't even know how.

Even though I warned you about the feels like ass part, achieving goals you've always wanted is pretty fun. It's so rewarding. But why do you want to create your extraordinary life? Make sure you like your whys. And then...let's get to work!

Chapter 2: Create an Extraordinary Mind

"If the only tool you have is a hammer, you will start treating all your problems like a nail." —Abraham Kaplan

I have always heard people say that mindset is so important. This is great in theory, but I had no idea how to actually apply that to myself. I didn't know how to change my thoughts or why it was important to do so. I didn't have the tools I needed to help me actually decide what to think or to realize that I didn't have to believe everything my mind offered me. It wasn't until I learned exactly what I'm about to share with you that my entire life changed. It wasn't until I learned these tools that I got my dream body, totally changed my relationship with food, made more money than I thought I ever would, got into the relationship of my dreams, traveled the world alone, and tons of other cool things like writing a freakin' book. I'm going to tell you everything that helped me.

And also, I love the quote I started this section with. To me, this means that if we have limited tools (or just one tool), we can't treat all problems well. We need lots and lots of tools. So please consider everything I teach you here. Put them into practice, even when it feels uncomfortable. But keep learning and adding new tools to your toolbox. No one tool works for all problems.

Once you've learned these tools, now you actually have to do the hard stuff and apply it to your own life. Don't just read this book and move on. Do the work. You can do hard things. You've got this.

Your Thoughts Create Your Reality

"Whether you think you can, or you think you can't – you're right"
—Henry Ford

I have no self-control around food.
I only like guys who don't like me back.
I don't want to work.

These were some things I used to believe were true. They were sentences I held in my mind and thoughts that I didn't question. I considered them facts. And little did I know, they were creating my reality. I was overeating all of the time and couldn't lose weight. I was chasing men and couldn't find a healthy relationship. I got fired.

People out there in the world are going to tell you that all of the things you do are what create your reality, that the actions I took are what caused all of that in my life. The food I was eating was the reason I couldn't lose weight. The men I chose created my bad relationships. The things I did at work caused me to get fired.

And while yes, technically the actions I took played a role, what you need to know is that your actions and the results in your life are all created by your mind and your thoughts first.

You can create what you want with your mind. That's the number one most important and valuable tool we have and I'm going to teach you how to make the most of it.

In order to change the way things are going in your life, you need to find the **cause** of the issues. You have to find the cause of why you're feeling unhappy, why you feel like you keep failing, and why you are not where you want to be in your life. So instead of having some wine to help with your anxiety, find the cause of why you're feeling anxious. Instead of starting a new fad diet, find out why you can't stop eating when you're not even hungry.

Many people will teach you how to treat the symptoms of your issues, but I think it's far more valuable to find what's causing them in the first place. And it will always (yes, always) come down to the way you're thinking.

The Model, created by Brooke Castillo, is what has helped me see this in my own life and change so many of the patterns I felt so stuck in. The Model is this:

C — Circumstance — The facts of the situation. These are provable.

T — Thought — What you think about the circumstance..

F — Feeling — When you think about the situation, how do you feel?

A — Action — What are all of the things you do (or don't do) when you feel that way?

R — Result — What is created in your life.

It's a formula that is taught in therapy, counseling, and all kinds of self-help. It's also a rule of the universe. Sometimes it's called the Cognitive Triangle or the Think Feel Act Cycle.

I like the way Brooke explains it because it made it really easy for me to apply to my own life and see directly how my own thoughts created the results I was getting and how I could change them to change my life.

I'll show you a few examples of how I changed my life using the model. This is how I used the Model when I felt like I had no self-control around food and couldn't lose weight:

C — The fact is, there are cookies in the kitchen and it's 9 pm

T — I think that I need those cookies and am not a person who can control myself around cookies

F — I feel impulsive

A — The action I take is I eat all of the things, eat when I'm not hungry, eat to avoid doing other things, eat in secret, hide, and obsess over wanting to lose weight

R — The result is I have no self-control

I ate the cookies because I felt impulsive from believing I had no self-control around food. And then eating the cookies just confirmed what I believed, that I had no self-control around food.

It's super important to see that it's never the circumstances around us that creates the results in our life. It's ALWAYS the thoughts we have. The cookies in the kitchen at 9 pm didn't cause me to overeat. It was my thought that I cannot control myself that led me to eat them. I believed that thought and it is what led me to eat the cookies.

I used to think it was just a fact that I had no self-control around food. And the more I thought it, the more I caused myself to go out of control. The Model helped me to see that. It helped me to see that my thoughts were creating my overeating. It helped me see the true cause of this issue. And the best news was that I had control over my thoughts and could change them.

So once I found out what exactly was creating the result in my life that I *didn't* want, I could create a new Model to create the result in my life that I did want.

C — The fact is, there are cookies in the kitchen and it's 9 pm.
T — I think that I am in control.
F — I feel confident.
A — My action is instead of eating cookies, I do something else I enjoy.
R — The result is I am in control around food.

I legitimately used to say "I am in control" out loud around food. It helped me so much. It changed the way I felt and the things I did. I didn't even fully believe it all of the time, but just saying it helped me so much.

There was one night when I was in the kitchen pouring a giant bowl of cereal at 11 pm. It honestly felt like food would just serve itself and I was some kind of zombie just uncontrollably eating my way through the kitchen, eating until I was physically sick. But then I remembered that thought. I am in control. I paused....oh. If I'm in control, why am I doing this? I'm not hungry. I don't even actually want this nor do I need it. I poured it back into the box and went to bed. I learned to change my thoughts, and it changed my life.

I'm going to give you some other examples of this, and I want to encourage you to try some Models for yourself.

C — The fact is I haven't had a boyfriend for three years
T — I think that I only like guys who don't like me back
F — I feel self-pity
A — The action I take is that I chase guys who show little interest and end things with guys who have too much interest in me
R — The result is I don't have a boyfriend and I keep chasing the wrong guys. I also begin to not even like myself when I behave this way.

And then, I worked on changing the way I was thinking and everything changed.

C — The fact is I haven't had a boyfriend in three years
T — I think that it could be really fun to date someone totally different than usual
F — I feel curious
A — The action I take is that I stop pushing away the guy that really likes me
R — The result is I do have fun and am open to dating so much more, which ultimately leads to a wonderful relationship

Here's another regarding creating a business.

Here's what happened when I let my mind wander without thinking on purpose:

C — I am making $0 in my business

T — I think I don't have time to have an amazing life and business

F — I feel unmotivated

A — The action I take is I think a lot about having a business, daydream, and compare my life to other people's lives

R — The result is I don't create an amazing life or business

Here's the Model I created on purpose:

C — I am making $0 in my business

T — I think I can figure out what a first step might be and it might even work

F — I feel excited

A — My action is to write a book and start an impossible goal coaching group

R — The result is I take steps in my business and things start working

Once your thoughts change, everything else in your life will change. They are the cause of everything happening in your life. While it can totally feel like thoughts are out of your control, I promise you have more control over them than you think. Training your mind is like training your body. At first it's super uncomfortable, you have no idea what to actually do, it feels awkward, and sometimes it hurts pretty bad. And then you get a trainer, and you do some research online, and find some people doing what you want to do, and learn from them. You keep going to the gym. You find a place to workout that actually feels pretty fun. You find a community of people on the same path as you are. You keep at it pretty much every single day. You get good at it. It becomes easier and you get super fun results in your life. Other people start to notice and they ask you for help.

In the gym example, you put the effort in and kept showing up and you changed and went through the pain and made it out on the other side as the person you wanted to be. Now you can continue growing. The same is true for changing your thoughts. It's a practice and you're going to get better as long as you keep going. In the beginning, it's supposed to be uncomfortable. Nothing has gone wrong if you aren't an expert at this immediately. You'll have to practice thinking new thoughts and believing new things and questioning why you believe what you believe about EVERYTHING. Awareness is everything. Then you'll figure out what you want to believe instead.

There isn't a list of perfect thoughts I can give you to believe. You get to make them up. They'll be different for everyone. You'll know it's working if you feel better and are able to take different actions more easily. That's how you know it's a better thought to believe. Helpful thoughts aren't going to make you feel bad. When choosing new thoughts to think though, I suggest you find ones that feel true. So if right now you believe you're fat and ugly, don't try to look in the mirror and think I'm skinny and gorgeous. This isn't going to feel true. You're smart. You're going to know this is some bullshit.

Instead try: "I have a body." "I have a human stomach that does cool things for me." "I think my eyes are pretty." You need to believe, or at least sometimes believe, your new thoughts. And then once you fully believe that new thought, move to an even more positive one. We call these ladder thoughts. We move up the ladder from our current thought to the thought we want to believe:

- "Maybe I'm not that fat."
- "Maybe I'm fat, and fat is still beautiful."
- "I have body fat and so does everyone else."
- "Body fat is okay."

With practice you can believe literally anything you want about yourself and your body.

I want to clarify that I don't think anyone should feel critical about their weight or believe that there is anything wrong with their body. I'm all for body positivity and loving ourselves where we're at. But in my experience, so many people struggle with thoughts like these and they typically make them feel terrible and then they go eat a pint of ice cream to feel better. I've definitely been there and it doesn't have to be that way.

I just want you to see how to first become aware of the thoughts driving your feelings, actions and life, and then have the option to slowly change the thoughts about yourself that you don't want to keep into new thoughts that will help you create a new reality and feel far better. Those sentences in your mind are where everything starts. I can't express how important it is to know what they are and practice being in control of them, and how important it is to start *talking to yourself* instead of just *listening to yourself*. Just because thoughts are popping up in your mind, it does not mean you need to believe them or that they're true.

Start noticing what's going on in your mind. Write down those thoughts. Put them into a Model and see how they are creating your reality. And then practice thinking on purpose. You'll be able to create a totally new, extraordinary reality.

Exercise: Changing Your Thoughts, Feelings, Actions, and Results

1. Do a brain dump of all of your thoughts on a particular subject. You can start with the prompt: "If I could change this area of my life, I would change..." and then just keep writing.

2. Pull ONE thought out of your brain dump. A thought is anything that we couldn't prove to be true. Something like "I'll never be able to do it" or "there's just not enough time." Something that if someone else heard you say it, they might be able to prove you wrong.

3. Put that thought into a Model. ·

C —
T —
F —
A —
R —

4. Now finish the rest of that Model. What are the facts going on when you think that? Put that in the circumstance line. Fill in the feeling line. When you think that thought, what is the one main feeling you feel? Then the action line. When you feel that way from thinking the thought, what are alllll the things you do? And

finally, the result. What does that create in YOUR life for YOU? Other people can't be in your result line. Hint: it might be oddly similar to your thought line.

5. Before you jump to the new Model that you want to have with the good thoughts and feelings and actions and results, let yourself sit with this one first. It's ok to have negative emotions. Don't beat yourself up. Your mind loves focusing on negativity to keep you safe. Nothing has gone wrong. Appreciate your mind for all it does to keep you safe and alive. Be willing to feel the negative before trying to get rid of it. Don't put sparkles all over the shit. Just notice it with curiosity.

6. Don't move on without completing #5. For real, it's important. But once you have done that and want to experiment with changing your Model, let's create a new one.

7. Keep the circumstance the same. If those same facts existed, how do you WANT to think about them, on purpose? If you truly thought that, how would you feel? When you felt that way, what would you do? And what would all of those actions create for you? Complete your new Model below.

C —
T —
F —
A —
R —

Yes, Feelings Are Actually Important

"Without awareness there is no choice." —Griff

"This is shame."

"This is shame."

"This is shame."

I kept repeating that to myself out loud while I was sitting in an Airbnb in Austin, Texas crying on a Sunday morning. I had woken up to a text message from the guy I went on a date with the night before that said he just didn't feel a connection with me.

I flew from California to Austin, Texas for a first date with this guy. We matched on Bumble about a month earlier when I was visiting Austin super briefly and were talking every day since then. He invited me to a concert in Austin. I thought he was the greatest thing ever (and by greatest I mean most handsome), and so I booked an Airbnb and flight to Austin for the weekend.

Once I read that message from him on Sunday morning, I couldn't stop crying. Why does this always happen to me? This was yet another case of the guys I like not liking me back. And now I was in Texas alone, with a full day of nothing to do and no one to hang out with. I just felt terrible. I kept thinking that this always happens to me and I'm never going to find someone who will love me. I kept thinking there had to be something wrong with me and I should figure out what that was.

I wanted to feel better. I remembered the advice I had heard before. Just name your feeling and be present with it. Say it out loud. So there I was laying in bed and I said:

"This is shame."

"This is shame."

"This is shame."

I let myself feel the giant black puddle of shame I was sitting in instead of trying to push it away. And yes, it made me feel much better. And yes, I did eat a whole pint of ice cream that night. (But Halo Top ice cream, so I didn't feel bad about it.)

I'm not a big feelings person (where my fellow Enneagram 7s at?!). I've never been one to cry. My mom asked me if there was something seriously wrong with me when I didn't cry at my great grandma's funeral. I just prefer to think I'm tough and don't need any of that feeling stuff, unless it's a cool feeling like happiness, excitement, or fun.

So if you're anything like me, you need to know that feelings are actually super important. Feelings drive absolutely everything we do. We do everything we do because we want to feel better or we don't want to feel worse. Think about it. We are driven by feeling better.

Not knowing how to manage negative emotions is exactly what is going to keep us stuck. It will lead to stress eating and gaining weight. It will lead to drinking the whole bottle of wine again even though you promised yourself you'd only have two glasses. It will lead to seven hours of screen time on your phone. It will keep you from creating the business or career of your dreams. It will lead to you spending all of your money on things you really don't even need or want that badly.

These are activities we do to distract ourselves so we don't have to feel the feelings: Restless. Anxious. Sad. Tired. Self-pity. Stressed.

If you don't handle the feelings, you'll most likely keep doing all of the things you don't want to do that are creating a life for you that isn't really getting any better. You have to get really freaking good at feeling everything you don't want to feel. When you want seconds at dinner but you're not even hungry, you have to get really good at feeling uncomfortable with having that desire and letting it be there without needing to do something to make it go away.

When you want more wine after you promised yourself you wouldn't have that third glass, you have to get really good at feeling restless while that half-full bottle sits there. You have to get good at letting yourself be anxious. Sad. Tired. It will feel quite terrible.

I can hear you saying, "But didn't you just tell us that our thoughts create our feelings, so why don't we just change the way we're thinking to feel better?"

Yes, changing your thoughts will also make you feel better. But changing your thoughts will take time. Putting sparkles all over the shit won't make the shit go away. All of the negative feelings will still happen because we are humans with human brains. Getting good at feeling any feeling is an invaluable skill because there will be certain times when you will want to be really sad and need to know how to feel that in a healthy way.

Okay so how can you become good at feeling your feelings? I love the acronym NOW coined by my coach, Krista St. Germain:

Using the NOW Technique

1) **Name it.** What exactly are you feeling? What is one word that names this feeling? Say it out loud. Repeat it out loud. Get really present with that feeling.

2) **Open Up.** Welcome it in. Focus on it. Focus on where you feel it. Typically we push negative emotions away and close ourselves off. The more you feel it, the better it will feel. The more you resist it and push it away, the stronger it'll come on. It's kind of like a really deep stretch that's so deep it's painful. When you breathe into it and focus on the stretch, it releases and relaxes. When you hold on tight, the pain gets worse and you don't make any progress in your stretching.

3) **Witness it.** Observe it like you're an outsider looking at your body. What does it feel like? Where is it in your body? Is it fast or slow? Is it heavy or light? How would you explain it to a robot who has never felt a feeling before? Get specific with exactly what it feels like, as if you had to explain the feeling to someone who couldn't feel.

Here's an example:

1. **Name what the emotion is.** I felt shame and said it out loud multiple times.

2. **Open up and let it in.** I laid there for a while and did nothing but felt shame. I didn't go on my phone or eat ice cream (until later that night) or do anything else to distract myself from the feeling. I just felt it. I didn't wish I was feeling another way to try

to push it away or freak out that it sucked. I just noticed where it was in my body. I felt it and breathed into it and was ok with just feeling it.

3. **Witness it.** Then I watched myself experience it and really noticed exactly what shame felt like. It was heavy. It was in my stomach and throat. It was slow and dark.

As you practice those three steps, you will get so much better at being ok with negative feelings. You will notice that less and less will you need to do things to make your negative feelings go away. You'll be able to be present with reality instead of needing to escape it.

Human Pain vs. Drama Pain

We are all going to have negative emotions, but you may be making those emotions worse because of the story you are telling yourself about them. .

Human pain is the pain of the facts. It's the pain we should be feeling because it's simply naturally painful. For example: trauma, relationships ending, people or pets dying, world tragedy, or not showing up as the person we wanted to.

Drama pain is adding drama to the situation that makes it so, so much worse. It's the story you're telling. It doesn't have to be there. It's unnecessary pain you don't want to or don't have to feel.

For example, the person you are dating breaks up with you.

Human pain: I'm so upset this relationship is over. I'm really going to miss him.

Drama pain: I'm so upset he left me. There's probably someone else much better than me. I'm never going to be good enough. Did he ever even love me? I hate him so much.

When you're in emotional pain of any kind, look at the actual facts of the situation and then notice the story you're telling yourself about it. Do you want to keep that story? Is it helpful? Is it true? Many times we don't separate the situation from our story about the situation.

When I was in Austin, Texas after that date, I told myself a big story about how this always happened to me and there was something wrong with me and there was no one who would ever love me. And then there was the situation: a guy I went on a date with said he didn't feel a connection. Big difference. I was in drama pain. I repeated out loud that I felt shame, I opened up to it, I witnessed what it felt like in my body and got really present with it.

I realized I was in drama pain, and I decided I wanted to change my story about the situation, so I made a list of all of the reasons why this was actually a good thing that happened *for* me. If I was going to make up a story, I decided to make it a good one. Some of the things I wrote were:

- This is leading me closer to my person who will love me SO much
- Now I get to spend a whole day in the city with just me, doing whatever I want and enjoying my own company
- I found out that this won't work out sooner than later

- I still had a fun trip and it's a pretty crazy story to tell
- Someone better is coming
- This is happening just like it's supposed to
- This doesn't mean anything is wrong with me
- This is a chance to learn how to love myself better

This helped me feel the shame in the moment, and then get rid of my drama pain that was on top of the human pain. Then I went out to the pool, read, and had a me day. And also I ate a whole pint of Halo Top in bed...and didn't feel bad about a thing.

Life is going to have ups and downs. It's inevitable. It's not a bad thing when life gets hard. Just practice how to get present, feel, and sit in the uncomfortable. When shit hits the fan, I want you to feel in control of your life no matter what. I want you to feel capable of feeling absolutely any emotion so that you are confident that no matter what happens, you can feel the feeling and keep showing up as the person you want to be and live your extraordinary life.

Exercise: Human Pain & Drama Pain

1. Write down a painful situation.

2. Write for at least five minutes straight about this situation. Keep writing even when it feels like you don't know what to say. You can literally write "I don't know what to say." Just keep writing for those full five minutes, and keep going if you still have more to say after that time is up.

3. Take a break for at least a few minutes. Walk around. Love your dog. If you only have a cat, go get a dog immediately (haha). Drink some water. Take time to feel the pain of it instead of pushing it away or changing it immediately.

4. Come back to your writing and try to read it like you're reading someone else's story. Get curious about why their thinking is the way it is.

5. Underline anything that you think is human pain. It won't have any drama or exaggerations or stories to it. It will just be those hard, painful facts.

6. Circle any drama pain. This is where your story comes in. It seems true, but you can tell it's your mind making this part up. Logically, you couldn't really prove it as true, but it still is there and it still hurts.

7. Just notice it. You don't have to DO anything. Without awareness, there is no choice. Just become aware. Eventually you will become aware that you can choose just human pain. No drama pain required.

8. When you're ready to change the story, write a new one. How could it be possible that good will come from this? How is it possible that this might have happened FOR you? Re—tell your story, but make sure you're the hero this time.

Creating Emotion

"There's nothing inherently wrong or bad about painful emotions. They're just physical sensations in your body." —Kara Loewentheil

Ever since I traveled abroad to Cambridge University (my first trip alone abroad and the trip that gave me my travel bug) where I met so many girls who were also traveling solo, I stopped feeling afraid of going on trips alone. I found that so many people would commit to traveling verbally, but once it was time for the trip, they weren't really committed. I was done with waiting for other people to go with me, so I learned to just be okay with going alone.

I posted in a Facebook group one day looking for someone, anyone to come travel with me. Well, not even just to travel with me but to live with me in a small minivan for 10 days. I was visiting the South Island of New Zealand and wanted to share both the costs and experience with someone.

I was surprised when I found someone else as crazy as me willing to meet a stranger on Facebook and then sleep crammed in a minivan with them. And I was SO excited.

To many people this probably sounds absolutely insane. But to me, it was just exciting because that was the emotion linked to my perception of the situation, past experience, and ultimately, my thoughts. I was excited because I was thinking I would be safe, I would have more fun with a new friend, and I would have more money to spend on experiences on the road since I could split the price of the car and gas. I was creating the excitement I was feeling.

Remember when I said that our thoughts create our feelings? Always.

My experience of being excited was unique to me. If we lined up 10 people and told them they would be traveling with a stranger and sleeping in a minivan, they would probably all have different feelings. It's *never* the event that creates our feelings, otherwise we would all have the exact same feelings. The event occurs, we have thoughts about it, and then we feel. *We* create our feelings, not what's happening outside of us. We have so much more control over our emotions than we think.

The second the woman from Facebook mentally decided she would go on that trip with me, I didn't feel excited. Her decision to go couldn't have impacted my feelings. I only felt excited once I read her message telling me that she decided she would go with me (and I believed her). It wasn't the actual event happening (her deciding to travel with me) that made me excited, it was my mind (reading the message, believing that she would actually go, and all of my thoughts about this being a great idea) that made me excited. If it was the actual act of her committing that made me feel, it would have happened the second she made that decision.

Outside things do not create our feelings. We do. This is the best and worst news ever. This means that we get to create the feelings we want. In that situation, I didn't have to create excitement on purpose, it just naturally happened.

In other situations, I've learned how to stop feeling a certain emotion and start feeling a more desirable one instead. For example, I learned how to stop feeling sooo much uncontrollable desire for sweets and instead feel complete control around them and so much less desire for them. I totally changed the way I used to think about food. That was one of my biggest feeling accomplishments. You'll hear more about it soon.

If we want to feel love more, we can practice creating love more. If we want to feel peace more, we can practice creating peace more. If we want to feel more gratitude, we can practice creating gratitude more. And this also means we have no excuses to not start feeling how we want to more often. You can teach your brain how to think and feel. You are in far more control than it seems.

It's also okay to not be able to believe the thoughts you want to believe all of the time. Sometimes it will be extremely hard to feel love, peace, or gratitude. That's totally normal. Your brain has been running on autopilot for years and years. It's going to take daily practice over time to change it.

Exercise: Creating Emotion

You just started a new workout program. The first week you just naturally felt motivated and did all of your workouts and ate on your meal plan. It was challenging, but because you felt motivated and kept thinking about how good you would feel and how much it would be worth it, you kept going.

Now it's week three. Waking up at 5:30 am sucks. You're tired. You're sore. And somehow even though you've been following your plan, you gained a pound. You don't feel motivated in the slightest. You're gaining weight anyway, so you think you might as well just go get a donut for breakfast. It feels like nothing could make you feel motivated this morning.

Answer these questions to help you create the emotion you want to feel:

1. When was the last time you felt motivated? What were all of the things you were thinking that made you feel motivated?

Example: I'm so excited to make a change for the better. This is really going to change me and everything about me: how I look, how I feel, how I show up for myself and my family. So much good is going to come out of my new diet and exercise routine. It could even be kind of fun. I can't wait to feel so proud of myself for doing it. This is going to be the best summer ever because I'm going to feel so good in my own skin. I'm so ready to do this!

2. Do thinking those thoughts create the emotion you want to feel? If not, find the thoughts that create the emotion you want to feel. Make sure you actually believe those thoughts, otherwise they won't create emotion.

Example: Yes, just thinking and writing those thoughts down now made me feel motivated! I really do believe they are true.

3. Which of those thoughts that made you feel motivated last time can you use now, that are believable currently, that will make you feel motivated today? Are there any new thoughts you can add that could help you feel motivated today?

Example: *I'm still going to make a change for the better, even though it didn't feel like it this morning when I saw I gained weight. I could be gaining muscle, which actually means I am getting closer to my goal. Not every day is going to be easy, but following through for myself on the hard days is what is going to make all the difference. If I keep following my plan every day, I will definitely get closer to my goal. I am getting closer to my ultimate goal every single day. If I don't give up, I will definitely keep making progress.*

Your feelings always come from your thoughts, although sometimes subconsciously. You won't be perfect at creating emotion immediately. It takes practice and trial and error. But you will get there.

And on those days that no matter what you try, you still can't create the emotion you want, make the decision to do the damn thing anyways. Do the workout. Eat the vegetables. Hug your partner when it's the last thing you want to do. Pay it forward. Sometimes you have to take the action even when you don't feel like it. That's exactly when you need to get up and do it. Especially when you don't want to.

When Action Creates Your Reality

"Well done is better than well said." —Benjamin Franklin

You just learned about how your thoughts create your feelings, which drive your actions. That is the way our minds work. But sometimes, you just can't think yourself out of a shitty feeling. Sometimes it's just there to stay for a while.

Your feelings physically affect your body. Sometimes they don't just go away with the change of your mind. I've found that sometimes I need to take action to change my reality. It's the opposite of all of the mindset work I've learned, but it absolutely works for me which is why I need to share it with you.

In this case, the actions I need to take always sound terrible in the moment. Sometimes that means cuddling my boyfriend when he's driving me absolutely insane. Sometimes that means working out when it's the last thing I want to do. Sometimes that means taking a shower when I'd rather just be gross and lazy.

It doesn't have to be huge, but those little things that I never want to do in the moment make a huge difference. They help me change the physical state my body is in.

When my boyfriend and I are fighting, we both need touch. We both need comfort because usually we're both feeling hurt. Neither of us are really in the mood for hugs and cuddles and love, but that's when I try to do it. When we hug, I feel more connected and loving. It changes the way I feel. It probably changes the way we both feel.

Today was a perfect example. I did nottttt want to go workout. I knew it was going to be a hard one. My activity for the past two days only included walking and stretching and I wasn't ready to go lift heavy weights and double my heart rate with whatever terrible cardio was in the cards. I had also spent the last couple days doing fun things and therefore eating a lot less healthy than usual. But I knew it was so important to just go take the action when I felt lazy. After the workout, I felt so much better AND I've eaten really well all day. I didn't create any motivation for myself to go do it, I just did it when I didn't feel like it, and my body just took over and got me back into gear.

I also didn't want to go shower immediately after the gym. I had 10 things that needed to get done today that felt more urgent. Yes, I'm one of those nasty people that can workout and chill in workout clothes for a while. Gross, I know. Stinky crew for life. And then I got myself to shower and put a cute outfit on (I'm also the kind of person who is more than happy to change from dirty workout clothes to clean workout clothes because leggings are forever the best pants). And after that, I sat down and got stuff DONE. It was the most productive part of my day. I got ready, so I felt better. And therefore my mind was in a much better place to be productive. I didn't try to think my way out of it. I knew what I needed to do, and I just did it. Then I felt better.

What's really happening is that the action is influencing new thinking, which is creating new feelings. And also certain actions create hormone releases that will literally change how we feel. That's the nitty gritty. But personally, in the moment, it doesn't feel like that. Sometimes it feels plain and simple — taking action makes me feel better.

Sometimes changing the way you're thinking is key. Other times changing what you're doing will change so much. Try it. Experiment. Find what works for you. Just keep going.

Feeling Pain

"When we argue with reality, we lose 100% of the time." —Byron Katie

Feeling pain absolutely sucks. It's terrible. When I was told that as humans we *want* to feel pain, I thought that was crazy. Why would I want to feel pain? I want to feel better....happier. Not pain. The one thing we seem to seek the most in life is happiness and feeling good. So how would it make sense that we want to feel pain? We feel enough pain as it is. I don't want to feel any more pain.

But the more I thought about it, the more I realized that I do want to feel pain. Human pain, at least. We can work on reducing drama pain so we're just left with the human pain.

I mean I don't want to feel pain often, but it is an emotion I want to feel. I want to feel human pain when someone I love dies. I want to feel pain when I lose a relationship that was important to me. I want to feel pain when terrible things are happening in the world.

That feeling of pain is what makes me take action. That pain drives me to make a change in my life, to tell people I love them more, to cherish every day, to speak up when I see terrible things happening, to know that happiness doesn't last forever, and to bask in that happiness when I have it. I don't want to be a nothing-but-happiness robot. I think there is more to life than happiness.

In fact, if we only had happiness, it would be pretty meaningless. It would be mediocre. Unexciting. The usual. It wouldn't be happiness. Pain is part of the human experience. It's there to make our human experience full. It's shitty in the moment, but it's necessary to feel. Pushing pain away will only make it worse. Pretending you don't feel pain will just make it build up (and this makes me feel like I'm crazy and am going to lose my mind.)

Pain isn't a bad thing. It's part of what makes the wild ride of a life we get to live. It's only a terrible thing when we push it away and make it into a terrible thing. Pain is. Happiness is. And when we argue with reality, we lose 100% of the time.

Choose Love Always

"What you think in your mind and feel in your heart is what you become." —David Cameron Gikandi

What's your favorite feeling? I like excitement, fun, thrill, connection, and most of all — love. Love just always feels amazing to me. I try to always cultivate the feeling of love in all situations, both for myself and other people. I can't think of a time when love wasn't the best option.

Choosing love doesn't always mean doing what the other person wants. Sometimes loving is hard to do. Loving can look like choosing love for yourself even if someone else doesn't get what they want. Choosing love can mean putting your wants and needs first and not people pleasing. It can mean loving others by asking how you can help. Choosing love can mean being honest even when it might not feel amazing to you or to the person you are talking to. There are a million ways to choose love. But I've found that choosing love can guide me on what to do and how to show up.

I can already hear you saying "But what about when love creates pain? I don't want to choose love always because love hurts. The more I let myself love, it feels like the more I am let down."

The thing I need you to know about love is this: Love is never the thing that hurts us. Pain is separate from love. Heartbreak is separate from love. You can have both love and pain, but love does not create pain.

Pain is created when we think something went wrong or something should be different. Pain exists because we believe: "It shouldn't have happened like this." "I miss them and I wish I was with them." "They should have done this differently." "They hurt me." We create our suffering. Love never does. And when we try to protect ourselves from pain, we also stop ourselves from loving fully. We can even create pain ahead of time by anticipating possible pain to come, like somehow expecting and feeling pain now will lessen the hurt later. It never will.

If a relationship does end, we typically *want* to feel that pain. Stay with me here. That's the human pain. That pain means you loved hard. It would honestly just be really weird to love hard and then not feel pain if that loving relationship ends. You can expect to feel pain after love ends because it's part of the human experience. We get to experience both the highs and lows. The love wouldn't be so incredible if we didn't have contrast. We often want to feel pain in those situations, even though it feels terrible. Pain lets our body know that we need extra care. You can do hard things and feel pain. And it will make you even stronger.

It can be scary to let yourself love. I used to be terrified of the pain of heartbreak. But I think letting yourself feel love is worth it every single time. Love is one of the best feelings. Don't stop loving hard because there might be pain. Don't let that fear hold you back from loving with your whole heart. Love is the best feeling. Choose love always.

Exercise: Choosing Love

1. Think of a recent time when you were in a situation that you might do differently if you could go back and do it again.

2. If you were to feel loving towards yourself in that situation, what would you have done differently?

3. If you were to also feel love towards the other people in that situation, what would you have done differently?

Not sure if the things you would do differently come from the feeling of love or another feeling? The actions will always be net positive. This means that there might be negative with the positive, but the positive will always outweigh the negative.

For example, I lied to my boyfriend for months about my past. It felt terrible, honestly. The choice that was most loving to both of us was to be honest. When I finally told him, both positive and negative things happened. It was good, but also bad. Overall, it was net positive. If you're not sure if you're feeling love or not, the actions you take from love will be overall good.

You won't be able to just immediately start feeling love all of the time. It doesn't work like that. But if you start looking back and evaluating what it might have looked like to show up in a more loving place for both you and others involved, you'll get better and better and loving in the moment, too.

Let's Go, Anxiety

"You can't stop the waves, but you can learn to surf." —Jon Kabat-Zinn

I can't talk about feelings without talking about anxiety. I get anxious. I think we all do. Anxiety, like any other feeling really, can come on unexpectedly and seemingly out of nowhere. You might just wake up and it's there to say good morning and may not leave for the entire day.

The most helpful thing I've learned about it is this. Take your anxiety with you. Let it sit in the back seat of your car and go along with you. Set it in your bag and drag that crap along with you. It's heavy. It sucks. It's going to keep making all kinds of annoying noises and poking at you until you think you might go crazy. But invite it along for the ride. It can come.

See it. Recognize it. Feel it. But you don't have to let it take control. Anxiety can sit in the back set. It can even ride shotgun if it's one of those days. But anxiety never drives. Know that in your soul, anxiety will never drive. It is not of legal driving age yet, it's just not safe, and you don't want it to. This is your car and you are the driver. You program the GPS. You decide what you get to do that day. Keep going, even though anxiety will be the loudest, most obnoxious backseat driver. This is your car.

There still may be days where you can't seem to get anxiety out of the driver's seat no matter how much you try. It may stop you from getting up and going. But you are still in charge of figuring out how to put yourself back in the driver's seat. Maybe on those days you decide to just stay home and take care of yourself. Maybe you try tapping or meditation. Maybe you call your therapist or a good friend. If you think your anxiety is a bigger problem than just a negative emotion, definitely talk to a therapist to see if you need more help with anxiety. Maybe you go for a walk or give your pup lots of cuddles. Experiment and try what works for you. But don't expect it to just disappear all together. Anxiety is coming, and that can be okay.

I used to *always* get anxious when I drove. My breathing was faster, my stomach would get tight, and I felt terrible. It was always there when I drove. But I just started to expect it and accept it. I knew it would pretty much always be there. I stopped trying to force myself to not be anxious. It was just a time that anxiety would be with me. And then one day it went away. There wasn't anything I did to change it or try to get it to leave. I don't even know when it went away. But I stopped resisting the feeling, and it went away on its own. Maybe it will go away sooner if you allow it to be there, and maybe it will stay forever. But what if you could be ok with having the anxiety there instead of trying to get it to go away?

Let's go anxiety. Fear, depression, and grief, you can come too. I'm still getting out there and getting stuff done. This is my journey and I'm driving.

The Important Part

"To grow yourself, you must know yourself." —John C. Maxwell

Ok, I need to say this. Something about this chapter has made me feel a little off. All of this stuff I'm talking about absolutely changed my life. I feel in control of every part of my life for the first time ever. I accomplished huge goals that I truly never imagined I would accomplish using the tools and techniques I have talked about here. But please, never ever use this stuff against yourself.

Never try to force yourself to feel better if you don't want to feel better. Do not blame yourself for feeling bad by somehow believing you are creating or manifesting the bad feelings. It's what your brain is designed to do. You're supposed to feel shitty a lot because of how human nature functions.

But if you feel shitty and still want to get shit done, I hope the techniques that I taught you help. And if you feel shitty and you decide you want to do nothing for the day and just feel sorry for yourself and this is what feels right to you and you're not going to feel guilty about it, by all means do nothing.

I love doing nothing. (I used to hate doing nothing but that's a story for later.) Don't feel guilty for the thoughts you've chosen. It's not beneficial. It just makes you feel even worse and then makes you choose more crappy behaviors that will likely start the guilt cycle over again. Use these techniques when they are helpful for you only.

Seeking Discomfort

"Discomfort is the currency to your dreams." —Brooke Castillo

You've heard all of the self-help gurus talk about discomfort. Discomfort is important. The practice of becoming comfortable with feeling feelings is what helps us sit in discomfort.

Are you actively seeking out discomfort? Are you building your mental toughness? It's something most people aren't doing. It doesn't feel good at all. But it's the most valuable skill you can create to help you get through anything life throws at you and to create an extraordinary life.

This means still going for a run even though it's raining outside. It's staying up late to get your daily tasks done even when you'd rather just have some wine and call it a night. It's having a super difficult conversation and being willing to admit when you're wrong. It's telling that person you like them when you have no idea how they feel about you. It's traveling alone around the country in a van when it feels terrifying.

Our brains are great at warning us of potential danger. They warn us when we get too close to the edge of the cliff to take that perfect Instagram photo (this isn't the kind of discomfort we want to go towards, of course). And our brains also warn us when we do anything that could risk us getting kicked out of our community, like breaking the status quo. While our brain absolutely protects us from real dangers, it also does a great job to protect us from perceived dangers that aren't truly dangers to us , like trying something new or being vulnerable. This is why it's so easy to stay the same. That's what our brain likes. But is that thing you want to do *actually* dangerous or is your mind just protecting you and trying to keep you where you're at?

When it feels scary, do it. When it feels totally out of your comfort zone, do it. When it feels uncomfortable, do it. That's your sign. That's your opportunity for growth. That's the currency you pay for your dreams.

Taking Massive Action

"Most people will give up and say it's too hard but you are not most people." —Jody Moore

Learning the importance of thoughts and feelings is vital. It will change everything, but only if you're willing to take the actions that are required along with them. Thoughts and feelings are so important because they set you up to take action. Sitting around and thinking all day is great, but you won't create the life you've always wanted without massive action.

So how do you know if the actions you're taking are "massive?" Often we do things that seem like the right action to take, but they are passive actions instead of massive actions. You can take passive action all day long and not get anywhere. The following chart will explain what the differences are so you can determine how to take the massive action that is necessary to reach your extraordinary goals.

Passive Action	Massive Action
<ul><li>The thing that's much easier to do</li><li>Feels productive</li><li>Feels much more fun and exciting</li><li>Doesn't require extreme discomfort</li><li>Passively planning things but not actually doing the big actions that will make all the difference</li><li>Won't get the results you're truly looking for</li></ul>	<ul><li>Taking huge, scary steps</li><li>Very uncomfortable and not very fun</li><li>Taking the action and following the steps of the plan you probably don't want to do</li><li>Much more likely to get you results</li></ul>

Examples of Passive Action	Examples of Massive Action
• Creating a meal plan for the week but not really following it • Creating a budget and never looking at it again • Buying another course to learn how to start the business you've always dreamed of and logging in twice • Messaging people on dating apps but not going on dates • Trying 3 different planners and then spending an afternoon bedazzling it to motivate yourself	• Saying no to the warm donut your partner just surprised you with because you have a meal plan to follow • Sticking to your budget when those shoes go on sale that you've been wanting • Offering the product of your new business to someone and asking them to pay you for it • Going on 200 dates in a year to find the partner of your dreams • Using the free, ugly calendar your neighborhood real estate agent dropped off on your driveway to plan the month, and then actually following that plan

Notice where the action you're taking falls — is it passive or massive?

Once you practice creating your thoughts and feelings on purpose, you'll be much more willing to take the big, scarier actions, to take massive action, to be willing to fail. And to create the extraordinary life of your dreams.

Later in this book, I'll give you the steps for how to plan your massive action so you know exactly what you need to do to reach your goal. For now, just notice. Are the actions you're taking toward your goal passive or massive?

Failure Ahead of Time & Redeciding

"I have not failed. I have just found 10,000 ways that won't work."
—Thomas Edison

I was scared. Scared of what people would think of me. Scared I was going to spend way too much money and never get it back. Scared I would regret it all. Scared people would think I'm a fraud. Scared of failure.

I wanted to help coach active people who felt like they couldn't stop overeating. That had been me, and coaching absolutely changed my life, my weight, my body image, my relationship with food, my confidence, and the way I thought, felt, and showed up in my life. Coaching helped me so much that I wanted to help other people in the same way. I felt like I had a secret and I wanted to share it with as many people as I could.

I started a coaching business: Abs are Made in the Mind. I kinda half-assed it because of my fear. The business made about $30k that first year, but there were also a lot of expenses I put into it. I still choose to see it as an absolute success. Then I got a job offer and stopped my coaching business to become an employee. I quit. I gave up. The job seemed better or safer, so I failed ahead of time, before any of the bad stuff happened that I was scared of, like people thinking I was weird for being a life coach, or people rejecting me. I just gave up.

What is something you've always wanted to do and why haven't you done it? For me, it was starting a business. A business where I could help women create the lives of their dreams, because I felt like I created that for myself. I created a life for myself that was better than I could have ever imagined. I wanted to share that. But when I tried it, I let fear stop me. I failed ahead of time. In the end, I still learned from this, and kept going towards the life I truly wanted.

Failure ahead of time is when you just quit so that you don't have to experience failure that is to come. You prevent actual failure by not even truly trying to succeed.

Failing ahead of time is different from making a confident decision to redecide or quit. I think there are very valid times to redecide and do something different. There is usually a negative connotation with the word quitting, but extraordinary people don't keep making the same decisions over and over simply because that's what they've always done. They constantly change course, figure out what's working, and do things differently.

Ask yourself why you want to quit and change course. Do you like your reason to change course? Is it because what you're doing is hard or because there's a better path that aligns more with your future self? If you had to make this decision again, would you still choose it? Would you choose it over again on purpose, or are you just choosing it because you've always chosen it? If you like your reason for quitting, such as this doesn't align with the direction you want to take your life, then quit and continue in the next best direction.

This is what happened when I lived in a van. I decided I wanted to be in a serious relationship instead, so I changed directions. That was not failing ahead of time, it was simply a redecision. I decided again and chose something different.

Logically, it doesn't really make sense to fail ahead of time, but our human brains do it often. Be aware of this human tendency. You're going to fail. Do you want to quit now, ensuring there will be no chance of the success you want, or keep taking steps towards your dream life and take the chance that you might fail later? If you fail ahead of time you cut off any chance for success. Even if there is only a tiny chance your dream will come true, letting it play out and giving it a shot gives you the chance. If you quit in advance there is a zero percent chance you can ever achieve the dream. Give yourself the chance. Keep going even when it feels hard. Trust that you're making progress. Remember why you're doing it.

Exercise: Are you failing ahead of time?
1. What is one thing you want and are currently working towards?

2. Why are you working towards it? Name a few reasons.

3. What are your fears around it?

4. What are three ways you are slowing yourself down or keeping yourself small and therefore failing ahead of time?

5. At what point would redeciding be a good idea for you?

Your Future Self

"It's not your job to like me — it's mine" —Byron Katie

I live in Laguna Beach, California in a house overlooking the ocean. You can hear the seagulls flying by and the crashing waves. When you walk onto the glass balcony, you can feel the crisp ocean breeze and a slight mist from the waves. There isn't anyone on the beach below. It's all for me. The sun is setting and I have the most perfect view of the sunset over the ocean. When I walk inside, there are giant floor to ceiling glass windows so it always feels like I'm at the beach. I can always see the sand and the waves. Everything inside is clean and white. It's simplistic. It almost feels like a hotel. It just feels peaceful. I can smell the essential oils throughout the house, and there is music playing on the Bose speakers in every room. In the mornings, I am wearing a black Lululemon workout outfit, leggings and a crop top. I have clean white shoes on. My body is lean, healthy, and so strong. After my workout, I change into a tight black dress and heels. I'm always a little overdressed. I go to work at my home desk. I am a best-selling author and I inspire thousands of people to create the life they truly desire. I speak, I teach, I write, I coach. I only work 20 hours per week and make plenty of time for myself and the people I love. I have five million dollars in my bank account, not counting the other investments I have. It feels so secure, generous, safe, proud. Everyday I feel extreme love and gratitude.

This is the future self that I visualize.

Our minds aren't very good at knowing the difference between reality and the things we imagine. The more super specific we become about visualizing our future self, the more we can become that person. We start to make decisions that align with who we want to be. We start to believe it's possible for us to have the life we truly want. We start to become our future self.

First, decide who you want to be. Really think about it. I like to listen to a guided visualization on Youtube every night before bed. It's called *5 Minute Guided Visualization Meditation To Manifest The Life of Your Dreams*. But I encourage you to even do more than that.

Really picture what you want in every area of life. Get as specific as you can. Think about the little details like the color of your nails and what you smell like. The more realistic of a picture you can imagine, the more your mind will think of your dream life as reality, and the faster you will be able to create it.

Over and over I heard about how important visualization was. I knew it was important. I visualized every once in a while. But the importance of visualization really hit me once I read *A Happy Pocket Full of Money:*

Infinite Wealth and Abundance in the Here and Now by David Cameron Gikandi. Visualizing is everything.

He teaches in the book that our life is just a series of things that we once visualized. I have my job because I previously imagined having it. I have my boyfriend because I previously thought about having him as my boyfriend. I am writing this book because I previously dreamed about writing this book. And maybeeee...just maybe, I have a little brother because when I was little I always talked about wanting a little brother. (He's my dad's son and I didn't talk to my dad until I was 15 so my dad never would have known I wanted a little brother.) Maybe it's a coincidence; maybe it's the universe doing what it does. That's the kind of stuff that REALLY blows my mind.

Our brain has a hard time determining what's real and what we imagine. Have you ever had a dream that you can't remember if it was real or not? Or you woke up in the morning feeling some type of way because your dream was so powerful, it made you feel things even after the dream was over? Our brain is so powerful. Just our thoughts can create extremely strong feelings. Visualization is powerful.

They've even done studies that show simply imagining exercise can tone muscle, delay muscle loss, and even make your muscles stronger. Wild, right? Our mind can literally create things that make no sense to us little humans. We think that lifting weights and eating protein create muscles. but apparently imaginations do, too.

By visualizing, we are literally creating our lives. We are telling our subconscious and the universe and God what we want. Do it consistently and do it often. It might just blow your mind.

Exercise: Visualize

1. Create a vision board. Yes, that's a real thing that really will help you create what you want. By looking at it every day, you are directing your mind and reminding yourself of your priorities. I have a vision board on my wall, on my phone background, and on my computer wallpaper. It's everywhere so I'm always seeing it.
   a. Here are some ideas of what to include: your ideal wardrobe, your dream home, the career you want, something that reminds you of your impossible goal, a screenshot of your bank balance (but with the balance you want), the car you want, the relationship status you want, your dream vacation, etc.

2. Do visualization every day. You can simply sit alone and visualize, listen to a guided meditation, or record yourself talking about your ideal life and listen to that. I've done them all, but I prefer to listen to a guided visualization or listen to my own personal recording.
   a. Search *5 Minute Guided Visualization Meditation To Manifest The Life of Your Dreams* to find the one I like to listen to.
   b. Record your own visualization on the Voice Memos app on your phone. Here are some ideas of what to include: my morning routine, my workouts and body, how I dress, how I

eat, travel, home life, my business, time management, family, friend, and romantic relationships, phone time, relationship with money and income, my car, my dog, and my future children.

How to Talk to Yourself

"We treat the things we love the best." —Bev Aron

"Lightweight baby!" "Ain't nothin' but a peanut!"

Ronnie Coleman, one of the greatest bodybuilders of all time, says this as he lifts weights that are in fact not light at all. I used to watch his videos with my friends in 2006 because we found it hilarious. But it all makes sense now. He was one of the greatest bodybuilders of all time because he knew how to talk to himself.

I found this skill to be most useful when I was running. Whether I was running one mile, 13.1 miles or 26.2 miles, the secret was in the way I talked to myself. People used to always ask me for running tips and my best advice is to not give yourself the option to stop and to occupy your mind the whole time. Don't think about running. Once your mind is busy thinking about things that aren't running, you'll then just kind of teleport to the finish line. The more you tell yourself it sucks, the more it's going to suck. With running, and literally everything we do, the secret to success is all in our minds.

The way we talk to ourselves is key. We have to practice talking to ourselves more than just listening to the shitty thoughts that naturally come up. I used to think telling myself I was amazing would turn me into a narcissist. But it's interesting because quite the opposite happens.

Think of a time when you thought you were actually amazing. How did you feel? What did you do? How did you treat people around you? I find that when I think about this I really start to believe that I'm amazing, that I am valuable, that I am actually really cool.

I feel great, confident, and loving. And I want to do amazing things. I want to compliment people. I want to donate money or buy gifts. I want to tell people I love them and write them nice notes.

When I believe I'm amazing, I typically start to do amazing things. When I think I'm a great runner, I typically run faster. When I think I'm an athlete, I typically eat in ways that fuel my body. You have to stop being afraid of talking to yourself in a positive and productive way. This doesn't mean we have no room to improve or grow. You can have both. You can talk to yourself like you love yourself and still notice and work on areas for improvement.

What if we talked to our kids the way we talk to ourselves? You're fat. You're ugly. You're not good enough. You don't get enough done. They probably wouldn't have a very great future hearing those things all of the time. You won't either.

Talk to yourself like you love yourself.

Exercise: Talking to Yourself

1. Take note of the things you say to yourself over a full day. Either bring a notebook with you all day or use the notes on your phone. Start the minute you wake up and continue all day. It might take a few days of doing this to even notice all of the times you talk to yourself.

   A couple hours of your notes might look like: *"Ugh I'm late."* *"These pants don't fit very well." "I shouldn't have done that." "I feel like a bad person." "I should just give up on that." "Dang, my muscles look great." "But she looks better than I do." "I should be more productive."*

2. At the end of the day, go back and look at your list. Rewrite any negative things you said to yourself in a loving way. Act like you had to say those things to a sweet little girl who you love so much. How would you say those things?

   a. *"Ugh I'm late."* → *"Next time I want to get up earlier so I have more time to get ready."*

   b. *"These pants don't fit very well."* → *"It might be time to get new pants! I want to make sure I have clothes that fit me."*

   c. *"I shouldn't have done that."* → *"Whoops! how can I do this better next time?"*

   d. *"I feel like a bad person."* → *"I don't like the way I acted. I want to change that by doing something differently going forward."*

   e. *"I should just give up on that."* → *"I know it feels really hard, but this is what I decided and I know it's the best thing for me, so I'm going to stick with it even when I feel like giving up."*

  f. *"But she looks better than I do."* → *"We're all on our own journey and she inspires me to keep going!"*

  g. *"I should be more productive."* → *"I'm going to get started now."*

3. After doing this for a few days, once you're able to start talking to yourself in a more loving way, notice how you feel. And notice if you start to show up differently towards yourself and others.

The better you get at practicing talking to yourself in a loving way, the better you will feel, and the more you will be able to show up as the person who you want to be.

Find Examples of What's Possible

"Inspiration exists, but it has to find you working." —Pablo Picasso

I was pissed. When reviewing a spreadsheet my boss sent to me, I saw it. One of my coworkers was making 10 times per hour what I was making. Ten freaking times. I couldn't believe it.

I immediately had all kinds of thoughts about how the work I do isn't valued enough and how I could possibly be 10 times less valuable than she was. But I had to stop myself. I knew where this was going. It wasn't beneficial to my life at all to be pissed about this. In fact, it was making me even less of a valuable employee. So I decided I would use it as an example of what's possible.

There are women out there in the world making shit tons of money. There are people out there who are creating businesses that are completely changing people's lives for the better. There are people rescuing tons of dogs that need good homes. There are people working just a few hours per week and making the amount of money they want to be making. There are people who are super present with their family and are extremely fulfilled at home. There are people who move their body in a way they love, eat in a non-restrictive way they love, and absolutely love the body they've created. There are people who believe they have the actual best relationship in the world. And there are people who get paid to travel the world.

They're all out there, doing things that might seem impossible to us right now. Our instinct is to be jealous—and even pissed like I was. But I promise you, those feelings are going to keep you further from the life you want to create. Use them as an example of what is possible. If they did it, you sure as hell can do it.

For years I absolutely idolized a woman who had taught me so much and created a life for herself I dreamed of. Over several years, I went from a complete fan girl to being her friend. I was invited to go for a walk with her, to go to her house, and to go out to dinner with her, her boyfriend, and one of her good friends.

In the Uber on the way to meet her, I literally felt like I was going to throw up. I was telling the Uber driver all about her and what a big deal this was to me. Hanging out with her was all I ever wanted. My stomach was in knots. I was so nervous and excited. Once we got to spend time together as friends, I realized something that changed my perspective forever.

She was just...a regular human. A human with an extremely successful business who was helping thousands of people, yes. But really, she was just a human. There wasn't anything supernatural about her. She didn't know a big secret to life that I was missing. God didn't sprinkle magic dust on her when she was born. She was just like me.

Extremely successful people aren't different from us. They just take action, always work on their mindset, and don't give up. They keep going.

You can do it too. You can create exactly what you want in your life. Other people have done it. Use them as an example of what is possible, not a reason why your life sucks. And get to work.

Exercise: Other People — They're Just Like Us

1. Make a list of a few people you look up to. This could be people like celebrities and authors, or people like your trainer at the gym or the girl you kind of know who seems like the most amazing person.

2. For each person, write:
   a. Something you admire about them
   b. Something about them that makes them just plain human (you might have to get to know them better to find this)
   c. How you are similar to this person

d. What part of you feels insecure, invisible, or underappreciated

e. What you're longing to do, be, or have

f. What is stopping you from it

g. How can you become inspired by this person instead

h. How can you turn it around and create something

Situation Beliefs

"Be happy, not because everything is good, but because you can see the good in everything." —Unknown

There are a few things called situation beliefs that you need to practice believing in order to create your best life:

- *Everything is happening exactly how it should be.*
- *This is happening for me.*
- *I'm exactly where I'm supposed to be.*
- *I always have my own back. No matter what.*

With that being said, there is also this thing many people, and life coaches particularly, will do. A thing I like to call making shit sparkle. Which is pretty much using those four phrases at times when they are not appropriate at all. You've experienced something majorly or minorly traumatic? (We all have). Those decision beliefs above do NOT apply. You do not have to believe it was supposed to happen or that it happened for you.

Shitty stuff has happened and it's important to realize it was shitty. Please don't force it to sparkle. Instead, look at it. Take it to a therapist to get more help. Have some grace with yourself and know that shitty things have happened to you, and you don't need to pretend it's okay. Use these beliefs for most situations in your life, but be sure not to throw sparkles over absolutely everything.

I was recently joking with my friend. We were on the phone for over an hour just catching up on all things life. She was telling me about the series of unfortunate events going on in her life, and I found myself spewing some of the phrases like I stated above. "Well...everything happens for a reason...or at least that's what they say?" I know she strongly believes in those phrases too, and we found ourselves questioning why we believe them at all.

When something bad happens, a break up, for example, it's pretty hard to believe it's happening for us or that the bad thing is supposed to be happening. But the way I think about it is that there is no benefit to believing something has gone terribly wrong.

When our mind believes something has gone wrong, it will start to look for examples of where things have gone wrong everywhere else in our lives. It's like when you start thinking about getting a new car, and suddenly you see that car you want literally everywhere. It's not because everyone suddenly bought that car, it's because subconsciously your mind is always looking for what you're thinking about.

Looking for everything that has gone wrong will not create the life you want, I can promise you that. Instead we have to ask our brain questions that will benefit us and we have to direct it to see the things we want to see.

"Everything that is happening to me during this break up is really happening for good."

Brain: "LOL no it's not."

"Yes it is. This is happening FOR me....to help me."

Brain: "This sucks, it's not helping you literally at all."

"Ok but what if it was helping me? I know it makes absolutely no sense right now...but just be still. Let's watch and see how this is happening for me."

Brain: "Fine!"

Three days pass.

Brain: "You're spending so much more time with your friends and family because this happened."

Brain: "Your relationship with your best friend has improved so much because of this."

Brain: "You're able to slow down and enjoy the little moments and things you do for YOU that you used to fly past."

Brain: "You seem so much more relaxed...even happier."

"YES! I told you it was happening for me! We just had to actually look for it to see it."

Ask your brain amazing questions that you want to find the answers to. Be willing to believe things that make absolutely no sense right now. Stop being realistic. Nothing extraordinary that happened was very likely or realistic. Just practice believing new things, things that will help you get to where you want to be.

Everything is happening exactly how it should be. This is happening for me. I'm exactly where I'm supposed to be. I always have my own back. No matter what.

I've read lots of stories of people who went through something bad, that ended up being a good thing for them. Here are a few of my favorites:

When I was sentenced to prison I thought life was over for me but...prison taught me more about myself than I ever knew was possible. I learned about who and what are important to me in life. It allowed me to reflect and really appreciate every single day individually. Prison is a horrible environment but a wonderful place to learn if you just open your mind to it.

My husband was fired as a high school basketball coach and the very next year was hired as an assistant college coach and won a National championship!

Had a condom break on April Fool's Day. Nine months later we welcomed our boy/girl twins.

Exercise: It Did Happen For You !!

Write your own success story. What seemed like a bad situation, but it ended up happening for the best?

How to Always Make the Right Decision

"Most people in life wait. They wait and put off the things they truly want to be in their heart for 'tomorrow', the mystical place where 99% of all dreams, human achievement and potential greatness goes to die." —Andy Frisella

I was terrified to make the decision. It kept me up at night. I had to ask every person I knew what they thought about it. I was afraid I was going to make the wrong decision. I wanted to leave home, invest about $40k in a van, and go travel the United States alone. There was so much that could go wrong, from buying the right van, to my safety. I just didn't know if it was the right decision for me.

This overwhelming mess of indecision was a familiar one. I was just as indecisive about buying a van as I was about who I wanted to date, what career I wanted to pursue, and what kind of donut I should get.

Making decisions didn't get easier until I learned how to make decisions. It's an actual skill and, yes, I just might put it on my resume.

Once you're familiar with the situation beliefs (or at least are willing to open your mind up and ask your brain how things could be possible), it's then time to make the right decision. Here's the secret to decision making:

You can never make the wrong decision. It's impossible. Go with your intuition. Your intuition trusts that you're always safe and doesn't need to logically rationalize things. It feels open and expansive. The decision you make is and will always be the correct decision. We know you made the correct decision because that's what happened. It was required for you to become who you are today. No matter what you choose, trust that it happened *for* you, and make the next best decision.

Now sometimes it may seem like that's not true. This is where the situation beliefs come in. You must decide to believe that everything is happening for you. You must always have your own back. Know that this is what's supposed to be happening.

You never have to regret another decision you've made. You never have to worry about making the wrong decision. Regret and worry are choices. You never have to choose them again. Have your own back. Make the promise to yourself right now that going forward, you are always going to do your best to make the decision that is right for you, and every single time without fail, it will be the right decision for you in that moment.

Each decision will lead to either winning or learning. And it was always the right decision.

Note: This may sound like me telling you to make crazy decisions and then convince yourself that it was a great idea. I understand that sounds nuts. But once again, there is one rule to doing this work and that is only to use it when it helps you, not when it hurts you.

As an example, I've used this in a situation where I took a job that I ended up finding out didn't work for me and I quit. I still trusted that I made the best decision in accepting the job because of what I learned. It taught me to practice letting go of things as soon as I know they're not the right fit. I could have used the situation against me though. I could have told myself, "See? You made the wrong decision. You're not good at listening to your intuition. There ARE bad decisions. You wasted your time and efforts on this and it ended up not working out." Queue 58 other reasons I could have told myself about why I chose the wrong thing and it was so bad.

For me, I've found this as an extremely helpful way to make decisions, never feel regret, learn, move forward in my life in a way that I'm proud of, and feel so much better. Even if something eventually feels like it was actually the wrong choice, it still taught you things, opened your eyes and further confirmed your belief about what is right for you.

Amazing Either Way

"If you believe it will work out, you'll see opportunities. If you believe it won't, you will see obstacles." —Wayne Dyer

He asked me to be his girlfriend. We had been dating for three months already and I still said no. I definitely liked him. I really enjoyed spending time with him. We had the best conversations ever and he made me feel like a queen. Why was I so afraid of the commitment?

I was about to leave on a trip for a few months. In the past, traveling was the way I had always gotten out of making any kind of commitment. If I just left, of course I couldn't commit to anything. It was always my easy out. (And absolutely some failure ahead of time on my part). So I asked myself one of my favorite questions ever.

"If it ended up absolutely amazing either way, which option would I choose?"

If I was single and it was amazing
OR
If I was in a relationship and it was amazing

If both options turned out to be absolutely amazing, which one would I choose?

The relationship with him was the answer. It was clear. I love having someone to love. If I knew it was going to be amazing, I'd be all in. And so I decided.

This question has helped me through a lot of decisions. Typically when I make a decision, my mind doesn't consider that either option will be amazing. It always assumes the options will be terrible. My brain immediately thinks of all of the things that could go wrong. (As human brains do because they're doing their job and keeping us safe.)

If I bought a converted van and traveled the US alone
OR
If I got an apartment and built my community at home

If I stayed in my current job

OR

If I quit and started a new career/business

If I invest in a new training

OR

If I use that money elsewhere

Flip it. What if either way, it worked out perfectly. Then what would you want to do?

Exercise: What if it was amazing?

1. What is a decision you are currently thinking about?

2. Write down both options you are deciding between.

3. Imagine both options could turn out amazing. Instead of letting your mind go to the negative that one of these options is going to go terribly wrong, flip it. What if either way, it worked out amazing? Then which one would you choose?

Intuitive Living

"To live is the rarest thing in the world; most people just exist."
—Oscar Wilde

My grandpa loves me a whole hell of a lot. People who love us sometimes tend to give advice that they've learned and sometimes it kind of sucks. It comes from love and worry and concern. They want the best for us. They want to keep us safe.

"You better enjoy it while it lasts. You can't live like that forever." My grandpa tells me this all the time. All. The. Time. He says it out of love, I know. But I always tell him that actually I can. I know that in my soul. He can't see that. He doesn't know that I have the desire to create an amazing life no matter what it takes and to not settle for the life our grandparents lived. We now have SO many opportunities and we can make money (a lot of money) in our pajamas. Life didn't used to be like that and it's kind of mind-blowing.

My extraordinary life is not going anywhere. I can live like this forever. I have a super freakin' fun life (which is a thought by the way, not a circumstance). I'm living out of my van traveling the United States. I've been to 27ish countries (lost track of my count.) I'm only currently working 20 hours per week. I do things that I love. All of the time. And while the old school motto was to just keep grinding to be successful and then have fun after you're 65, I'm not convinced.

When I was at Machu Picchu in Peru, out of breath from climbing tons of big, uneven, steps, I couldn't help but think: "Someone's absolute biggest dream is to visit Machu Picchu. What if they wait? What if they wait until they can't climb stairs very well any more?"

Machu Picchu is currently sinking and in the future will be closed to foot traffic. What if that person waits and they can't experience it the way they had always dreamt of? That breaks my heart. I'm not on this planet to live a life I don't love for 65 years and then try to start my life. It's just not happening.

in·tu·i·tive
Based on what one feels to be true even without conscious reasoning.

I like to call it intuitive living. Live the life you want, even when it makes no logical sense. The woowoo manifestation people are big on this. Do it even when it makes absolutely no sense. Keep believing in the big, extreme, extraordinary vision even when you have absolutely no reason to believe there is any way it's going to happen.

I'm not a manifestation expert yet, but what I do know is humans don't understand the role of energy that we can't even see and how it affects our world. Being in that high vibrational, dream life, extraordinary energy is what attracts more goodness to your life.

When I quit my $150k job, I had no doubt in my mind I was going to uplevel. That belief in myself is what created amazing future opportunities. Living intuitively involves trusting yourself fully. It is knowing that no matter what, you will make it happen, whatever "it" is for you.

Living intuitively involves listening to your desires and following them. Your desires are extremely unique to you and they are your path to living your exact life purpose. Your desires might seem crazy or unrealistic or not sustainable. People might tell you just that. Maybe you want to make art all day or rescue all of the animals. There are plenty of people making amazing lives doing those things. Find examples of people doing what you want to do for inspiration.

You don't have to settle for less. You don't have to settle for "enjoy it while it lasts." It's going to last. Trust that.

And sometimes it's going to be scary. Probably a lot of times. The minute you start trusting isn't the minute you're going to start receiving. It's going to take trial and error, failing, and risk. But as long as you keep going, you're going to get closer and closer to the life you want.

You don't have to believe "you can't live like that forever." You can. In fact, I believe every single year of my life is going to be better than the last. Because that's what I'm creating. And that's what I get to believe.

Try living intuitively and listening to yourself and what you really, truly want, even if it seems crazy, scary, and unknown. Don't wait to do it. Listen to your desires. They will direct you to the exact life you're supposed to be living.

Exercise: Listening to Your Intuition
1. At what times do you feel your intuition and know your desires best?

Some people write. Others go for long walks with no music or podcasts. Maybe it's a long drive at night, or your alone time in the shower.

2. When and where do you feel your intuition?

It's the voice that loves you. The voice that dreams big. The sometimes strong, loud voice that will tell you something even though there is no logical reason for it.

3. Notice when you can hear it and write down what you hear.

4. Start taking steps towards what it tells you. Do more of what lights up your soul. It will guide you to incredible things.

Chapter 3: Create an Extraordinary Body

"Don't wait on your weight to live the life you want." —Cece Olisa

"No, thanks. I don't like bread," I remember telling a new friend I was out to dinner with.

Obviously, I like bread. I love bread, but I didn't have the self—control to not eat it. The only way I could think of in that moment to stop myself from eating the bread was to just tell her that I didn't like bread at all. I couldn't have bread because putting any carbs in my mouth would have made me a fat cow, of course. If I had a piece of bread, I would know that I absolutely blew it would then it would make sense to have four more pieces of bread and all of the cookies I could find later that night.

I had some issues around food.

At the time, I wasn't sure if I had an eating disorder, but now I know what it was. I had orthorexia. Orthorexia is an eating disorder that involves an unhealthy obsession with healthy eating.

I wanted to lose weight and be skinnier. I never liked my body, even when I was working out three hours per day. I would literally do/try anything to lose weight. I also felt like I had no self-control around food, so I would always eat when I wasn't even hungry, and eat waayyyy more food than I needed. I would eat until I was sick. I would eat when I was bored. I would eat while doing homework or working to make it suck less. I would eat to avoid feeling things or to try to feel better. I would just eat. A lot.

Sometimes I ate a lot of healthy things, and sometimes it was a lot of super unhealthy things. I couldn't turn down free food. I hated wasting food. I was "always hungry" because I thought it was cool. I didn't want to be one of those "salad girls" because I had heard guys say they didn't like a girl who ordered rabbit food on a first date.

I used to eat spoonfuls and spoonfuls of Skippy peanut butter while I was babysitting because peanut butter was healthy and I couldn't handle babysitting without needing to distract myself with food.

I once went out to a family buffet brunch, ate literally the entire time, went home to do homework, and started eating again because I needed to be eating while I was doing homework to make it not so bad. I almost threw up that day from forcing myself to be so full.

I thought it was cool to be able to eat a shit ton and not be too overweight, meanwhile I was killing myself both in the gym and in my mind.

When I was living in New Zealand with the family I was nannying for, one day they decided to have a fasting competition. Who could not eat for the longest amount of time? Fasting has great health benefits so this challenge didn't have any bad intentions, and I was always up for an insane challenge. I would do anything to help me lose weight...you know, so I could love myself. I made it to about 36 hours of fasting. I woke up in the morning and walked upstairs. I started to feel really dizzy, and my host mom handed me a banana to eat and told me to sit down. That's the last thing I remember. I woke up on the floor looking up at the whole family standing above me because I had just passed out. That's the only time I've completely passed out on the floor. And it was to try to get just a little bit skinnier. Anything. Anything to be a little skinnier.

I didn't fully realize I had a problem when I was in it. I was proud of myself for being so educated about what kinds of food were healthy. I just couldn't understand why I didn't have an amazing body. And why I still hated myself. And why food seemed to have a weird control over me that I couldn't seem to overcome. As much as I thought I was smart and knew it all, I had a lot of learning and inner work to do.

Now I'm at a place where I feel like I have complete control around food. I'm confident that I can lose weight whenever I want to. I absolutely love my body. I eat all kinds of things I never would have let myself eat before. I don't overeat or eat to not feel my emotions. Food and how my body looks isn't a big part of my brain space like it used to be. Now I can put my energy into other parts of my life that I truly want to focus on. And in this day and age, surrounded by photoshopped Instagram models, I think we could all use a little help loving our body.

In the following chapter, I'll share my story and everything I learned along the way so you can get to this place, too.

How to Create Your Dream Body

"You have been criticizing yourself for years and it hasn't worked. Try approving of yourself and see what happens." —Louise Hay

I did intermittent fasting, keto, and calorie counting all at the same time. I tried Whole 30 and the military diet and paleo. I tracked macros. I had Pinterest boards full of healthy recipes and workouts to try. I knew a damn lot about nutrition and workouts.

I'm pretty smart. But I still couldn't lose weight. I couldn't love, or even like, my body. I thought about food constantly. I was obsessed. I was still looking for a way to lose weight. Little did I know that was the absolute last thing I needed.

I found another new program to try that promised weight loss: Stop Overeating. That sounded just like me. I knew what to eat, how to lose weight, and all kinds of diets. I just couldn't follow them or control my portions to save my life.

As soon as I started a new diet, someone would ask me to get ice cream. Or ask me if I wanted a cookie. A FREE cookie. I couldn't pass that up. Or there were leftover soggy graham crackers with cream cheese at the preschool I worked at that they were going to throw away. No one would be throwing away a soggy graham cracker with cream cheese around me. I would eat them all. Even though I just finished my breakfast. (Yes, disgusting, I know.)

In this Stop Overeating class, I learned all about how to solve the cause of my overeating, and it was not just trying new diets every Monday. I was overeating because I truly believed:

- There's something wrong with me.
- I have no self-control around food.
- I can't lose weight.
- I don't want to waste food.

I was overeating because I ate to avoid feelings like:

- Anxiety
- Boredom
- Stress
- Awkwardness
- Restlessness
- Literally any other feeling

I was overeating because I had some really shitty sentences in my mind about myself and who I am, paired with the fact that anytime shit got uncomfortable, I absolutely couldn't stand it. Learning that is what changed my relationship with food, my body, and my life.

I figured out that the more I told myself that I had no self-control, the more I binge ate. I started practicing feelings that were uncomfortable and not eating to avoid them. I practiced saying no to free food, and...I didn't even die!! I did a lot of work discovering the story I was telling myself.

I learned that I, in fact, was not born with both blue eyes and an obsession with sugar. I could change how I felt about sugar and food, and I was in control of it fully.

The following section is for people who feel like they have a bad relationship with food or bad body image. If what you're doing is working, you don't need to fix it.

Here are some action steps to take to learn how create an extraordinary body:

1. **Discover your relationship with food. Take time to journal about the way you feel about eating, food, and your body. Write down all of the rules you have about yourself, what you should and shouldn't eat, and what you feel like is impossible for you.**

I truly felt like it was just impossible for my body type to have a flat, toned, stomach. Later on I found out that absolutely wasn't true.

Once you have everything written out, you can see all of those thoughts that seem like just plain truths about yourself are what are blocking you from creating the exact body you want. All of those sentences in your mind are keeping you exactly where you're at. They're keeping you stuck. They are the keys to unlocking the body and relationship with food that you want.

I know, you're thinking that your food rule about how you should never eat sugar is actually helping you create the body you want. And yes, logically that could make sense. But what usually happens is that when you think you can never eat sugar, you then start feeling deprived and then eat a ton of sugar. Sound familiar?

If not, maybe that's working for you. But in most cases, it seems like a healthy rule until we find out it makes you feel bad or restricted and then there is a net negative result from it.

Again, please only take the things that are helpful to you. Everyone is different. I know people who have completely cut out sugar and are doing amazingly well.

When I tried to cut out sugar, I was secretly pissed that all of the Instagram influencers with incredible bodies could eat sugar and look like that and I couldn't. So I'd binge eat at 11pm, which just made it even more true for me that I couldn't lose weight.

2. **Go through your list and highlight every sentence that doesn't make you feel great.**

Honestly, it might be all of them. Highlight things like "My body doesn't do well with carbs." While it probably feels true, it also doesn't feel good to think that.

Highlight it if part of you is bummed about it or wishes it was different. You don't need to highlight any sentences like "I love my glutes." or "I'm proud of myself for eating a healthy breakfast everyday." But since you're a human with a human brain, and we tend to focus on the negative pretty much always, I would guess that you don't have a ton of awesome sentences like that.

3. **Plug your highlighted sentences into the think → feel → do cycle. The think → feel → do cycle originated from Cognitive Behavioral Therapy and is similar to the Model I taught earlier, but simplified. When you think that sentence, how do you feel? When you're feeling that way, what do you do?**

When I think "my body doesn't handle carbs well," I feel restricted, and then sometimes I don't eat carbs because I think I shouldn't, but then later on when I'm alone, I eat everything in sight. Sometimes it may seem like when you are living your food rules, they're helpful. Sometimes when you think sugar is bad, you skip the sugar. But then what? What else do you do? If you're feeling like you have any kind of issues around food, there is probably some kind of negative action resulting from the thought and negative feeling that accompanies it.

That was my biggest work when it came to food and my body image. Realizing that the thoughts I was having that I thought were helping me were actually hurting me. I had to completely change the way I was thinking.

I thought that the more I hated my body, the more I'd motivate myself to change. But all that happened was I treated my body like something I hate. We treat the things we love the best.

4. **Try planning your food ahead of time. Either the night before or the morning of, plan exactly what you're going to eat that**

day. Write it down. It can be super specific like 4oz chicken and 1 cup of rice and ½ avocado. Or as simple as three meals with no snacks or dessert in between.

Note: Only try this if you need help. If you already have a healthy relationship with food, like your body, and are healthy, keep doin' what's working.

The reason that planning ahead of time is so important is because it uses our prefrontal cortex. This is the part of our brain that separates from animals. It's great at planning for goals and thinking clearly. This is the part of our brain that makes the best decisions for us. This is why it's super easy to say "diet starts tomorrow." This part of our brain wants an amazing future for us.

And then there's the part of your brain that loves immediate gratification and immediate pleasure. There's nothing wrong with this part of our brain. It is what kept us alive historically. It helped motivate us to do a lot of hunting and gathering just for the pleasure of food. It made us want more, more, more food, just in case we couldn't find any. Our ancestors were probably amazing binge eaters and that's why they survived. They needed to eat all of the food when it was available. But now our brain is confused. It still thinks we need to eat everything immediately to survive.

When we plan, we use our prefrontal cortex to make the best decisions for us tomorrow. I also suggest making your plan something you *want* to follow, something that would be amazing to follow and you'd be excited to eat that way for the rest of your life. Quick fixes and nothing but chicken and veggies is not sustainable. It is not creating good long-term habits. Create your plan like it's something you'd like to follow forever.

5. Follow your plan.

This is the hard part. This is the part where you're going to feel super uncomfortable. This is when you're going to literally want to eat anything besides what is on your plan. And this is also the part where you learn to build so much trust in yourself and become a person who always does what they say they are going to do. That is the most important thing I learned from following my plan.

I had always been a person who couldn't trust myself around food. Now I absolutely can. I had to feel a lot of discomfort to get there. But would you trade having some discomfort for absolute trust in yourself? It's so worth it.

The other important part to know is that yes, it's going to feel uncomfortable sometimes, but when that happens, always go back to what you're thinking. What am I thinking right now that is making me feel deprived? Once you identify this, then you can work on changing that thought in your mind. You never have to feel deprived. Deprivation is a feeling that is created by the way you're thinking, and you get to think anything you want. You won't feel deprived around ice cream if you believe dairy is harming your body and you truly don't want to have that kind of dessert. But you might feel deprived if you believe you can't have ice cream because carbs before bed is a big no-no. Deciding that you don't want certain foods with a healthy why will not create deprivation. Decide what you want to eat on purpose and with intention, and create your meal plan around that.

6. Make any adjustments and keep going.

It's kind of like a science experiment. There is no one perfect diet that is going to work for everyone. You get to figure that part out. Things aren't going to work. You're going to gain weight sometimes. You're going to forget to even create a plan sometimes. That's okay. It's not supposed to be perfect. Just adjust, and keep going. Don't add any drama to it. It doesn't mean you'll never lose weight or have the body you love. Adjust. Keep going. Repeat.

Did We Forget About Health?

"Remember that our bodies are always changing, and that's okay. What's really unhealthy is trying to fit into an unrealistic norm of what is seen as perfect." —Olakemi Obi

I think it's really interesting to look at why society is so in love with being skinny. Why do we think that skinny is better? Why are we willing to go through super unhealthy things in order to get skinnier?

Aphrodite, the goddess of love and beauty, has belly rolls. Having stomach rolls in the past was considered beautiful. It was the sign of someone who was well—fed and didn't need to do strenuous work. Belly rolls were a sign that a woman was healthy, rested, and was of a higher class.

Now things are a little different. Society (generally as a whole) now sees thin as beautiful. It shows that someone has time to go workout, has the money and time to eat healthy, and cares about their body. We value thin bodies because we value health and we associate thinness with healthiness.

But that's now so far from the case. So many people who are thin aren't healthy at all. Studies have shown that at least nine percent of the population has had an eating disorder. I'm sure that number is lower than the actual truth. We are so obsessed with being thin that we throw our actual health out the window.

The more I learned about health and surrounded myself with "healthy" people, the more I learned that they tend to drink a lot of diet soda, energy drinks, and zero calorie pancake syrup filled with chemicals. (Full disclosure: I used to be the person who would never put any of that fake stuff in my body, and now I don't see any food as terrible and do eat all of the things in moderation including diet soda and sugar free syrup.) The more I got to know girls who from afar looked like they just naturally had the best body, the more I realized how many people do have eating disorders and unhealthy relationships with their body and food.

I think the goal should be our health. I think the super thin body might not always be the healthiest. I think one's body and what it looks like really is much less of a reflection about our health than it might seem.

Question why you want to be thin so badly. Most people say they just feel good. If you could feel your best and not be super thin, would you want that? Would you still think that was extraordinary? Just consider why your idea of an extraordinary body is what it is.

My ideal body used to be super thin, abs, super toned, Instagram model looking. And then I got that body and realized that's not actually what I wanted.

Through that experience I learned a lot. One thing I learned was that my extraordinary body is super strong, it isn't the leanest body around, it has enough fat for my body and hormones to function properly, it feels amazing, it eats in a way that feels completely controlled but also free, and it makes me so incredibly proud. Oh, and it looks amazing. But in order for me to learn what was my ideal body, I had to do the absolute hardest thing I've ever accomplished in my life.

My First and Last Bikini Competition

"Having a flat stomach doesn't make you more worthy. It won't make you happier or more successful." —Rae Ann Langas

I felt for the first time in my life that I had self-control. I felt like I could truly follow a meal plan. I had never felt like that for as long as I could remember. I wanted to do something for myself that would prove to myself that I truly could follow *any* meal plan. I decided to do a five month "prep" for a bikini competition. This is a full five months of eating and working out according to a very specific plan with very little wiggle room for days off or cheat meals.

I hired a coach who would provide me with the meal plans and workouts that I would follow exactly up until I got on the stage. I was careful with who I chose because I wanted to do my prep in a healthy way. I didn't want to go with a coach that would starve me or who cared about what my body looked like more than they cared about my health and mindset through it all.

My workouts usually took about three hours to complete (but maybe it took so long because I was taking selfies during my workouts and practicing handstands after). I was eating six meals per day and weighing every single thing I put in my mouth. I was still eating a good amount of food, but it was just super healthy and basic. I didn't use sauces or anything fancy. I ate to live and to feel good and become stronger and healthier. I was tracking my water intake to make sure I was drinking a gallon per day. I was taking all kinds of supplements. A couple of times whatever I took caused me to break out into a rash after I took them and I could never figure out what had caused that.

During this time of my life, my meal and workout plans came first. I went out to dinner with friends and family and brought my own little tupperware with my tiny meal. If I wanted to go on a weekend trip, I spent time making and measuring all of the food I needed for the weekend. I was committed.

There were days that were really freaking hard. There were days (lots of days) that I cried. It was a lot. I had given up my typical way of avoiding my emotions and I was now just feeling them. My first love and I broke up while I was on prep for my competition. I transitioned from living in Australia with him to moving back home with my mom in California. I remember going to the gym the morning after we broke up and just crying on the treadmill. And I finished that damn workout. I put a mud facemask on and lay on the bench in the women's locker room and just cried. But I didn't go and eat a pint of ice cream to feel better. I stuck to my plan. That was a huge win and I was so proud of myself.

I had tons of wins along the way, from getting in all of my workouts on days that were super busy so I had to stay up late, to always being prepared and bringing my own food anytime I went out, to learning how to not feel bad for myself because I was choosing to follow a meal plan without making compromises. I made it work. I had no excuses. I didn't give myself any option other than to just get the shit done.

And then five months later, I competed in a bikini competition. Many of the girls looked like they felt terrible on the morning of competition day. They probably did. They were sitting on the ground backstage waiting for their turn.

We weren't supposed to drink much water at all that day or the day before. On show day, we dehydrated ourselves so we looked leaner. That's the unhealthy part of competitions. That last week isn't about health at all, it's about seeing where you can get your body. It wasn't something I planned to put myself through again, but I was still excited to see what my body was capable of.

We also couldn't eat much. For breakfast the day before my competition, I ate ¼ cup of completely dry oats (again because I had to restrict my water) and a few ounces of tilapia. It sounds absolutely disgusting, but anything tasted good when I was that hungry.

Everyone had a super dark tan. So many people ask me why the tan is so dark and it's because the stage lights are so bright, it really washes you out if you're not tan. I still think it looks ridiculous, but hey, that's part of the game.

I wasn't one of the girls who looked miserable. I was so excited. But something strange did happen. I wasn't excited about getting up on stage to compete. The day had come and it wasn't even very exciting anymore. It wasn't because I had stage fright (even though naturally I was nervous AF to walk on stage in huge heels basically naked to show off my body). I wasn't excited because it wasn't walking up on that stage that mattered. What mattered was that I freaking did it. I followed a meal and exercise plan for five full months. I completely transformed my body and created a body I truly never thought would have been possible for me. I learned to do really hard things and fully trust myself. I knew I could accomplish what I set out to do. And I did it in a way that didn't have me messing up my mind around food even more.

Standing backstage I was thinking a few things:

- Holy shit, I did it.
- This is so fun that I look like this!
- Hm, I still have that little lower tummy bump that I've always had (sidenote from the future: that was pretty much the only fat left on my body and it was there to protect my future babies...)

- I still don't like this picture of myself.
- I'm so proud of myself.
- Can I go home now?
- I thought I'd be happier once I got this body I wanted so badly.
- I'm so glad I did this.

Was it hard to transition back to eating not in preparation for a competition? For sure. But overall, I'm so thankful for the experience and SO much good came from it in my life. I'm still so proud of my commitment and determination.

I don't recommend doing a bikini competition in order to help you create a healthy relationship with food and yourself. That part has to come first. The competition was the biggest test of my relationship with food and myself. There are pieces that aren't healthy about it. You'll create a body that is probably the leanest you'll ever be, and it's most likely unattainable to keep in a healthy way. If you're interested in competing, I think you need to be in a really good place already to be successful.

I've heard stories of bikini competitors who would just binge and binge on cupcakes. I've heard many stories of women starting to train for a competition but not being able to follow the plan and needing to quit. It's not an easy sport. It's all mindset.

I thought achieving my goal was going to be so much different than it was. I thought I'd love myself all the time once I had that body. I thought my relationship would get better and my boyfriend would love me more (we broke up during my competition prep). I thought I'd be more successful on social media and that I'd be able to help so many more people because I had lost weight. I thought I'd be happy. I thought I'd love myself. I thought other people would love me more. But none of that happened.

Yes, I was extremely proud of myself. Yes, I repaired my trust in myself to do the things I said I was going to do. Yes, I learned that I could in fact follow a plan without giving up. But so many things that I thought would change by accomplishing this goal and having a thinner body just didn't happen. Skinny didn't equal happiness.

Too Skinny. Too Fat. Too Strong.

"I can't give you a sure-fire formula for success, but I can give you a formula for failure: try to please everybody all the time."
—Herbert Bayard Swope

"Just don't get too strong. It doesn't look good."

"You've gained some weight, haven't you?"

"Better watch what you're eating..."

"Buh-buh-bu-licia."

"Wow, you eat a lot!"

"Are you on drugs?"

"I don't like a girl with muscle."

"She just doesn't eat anymore."

All of these things have been said to me at different points in my life, mostly by people who love and care for me. Sometimes what is said out of love sure doesn't feel like love.

People are going to say things that suck. They're probably going to comment on your body at one point or another. Someone is always going to have something to say.

Here's my best advice. You decide how to think about you. If you're worried you're too skinny, too fat, or too strong, when someone else says it, it's really going to hit you right in the feels. It hurts when we believe that whatever a person says to us might be true. If you believe it might be true, it's going to hurt. Sometimes comments about me being fat really, really hurt me, because I thought I was fat. At other times, comments about me being fat didn't bother me. I remember saying once "Good thing I don't believe I'm fat because that would have really hurt me if I did." The person who said it assured me it was totally a joke because of course I wasn't fat. Stop listening to what other people tell you about your body and decide what YOU think about your body.

You have to start doing the work to change the way you're thinking about yourself and your body. You are the only one that can make that change. It's going to be a process and it's not going to happen immediately, but being committed to changing the way you think about yourself is what's going to change everything.

Do you ever look at a gorgeous model and think "if I just had that body, I would be able to love my body?" I've thought that. But the crazy thing is that so many models truly hate their bodies. I would go so far to say they might even hate their bodies more than just the average person.

It's not the body you're in that determines if you love your body. That part is 100% up to you. You get to decide if your body is extraordinary or if it's horrendous. You are literally the only one who gets to decide.

Fun fact: When I calculate my BMI, it tells me that I'm overweight. I've also taken body scans that tell me that I'm "at risk." At risk for what? Looking amazing? It's wild. I have such a healthy and thin body, and these scales are telling me that I'm overweight and at risk. I think my body looks incredible and is absolutely extraordinary.

Don't let other people tell you how you feel about your body. Don't let the made up calculators decide. Don't let your mind run around unsupervised and think all of the shitty thoughts that are being pushed onto you. YOU decide for yourself.

How do YOU want to think and feel about your body?

How to Love Your Extraordinary Body

"One of the greatest mistakes you can make in life is assuming all your thoughts are true." —Jon Acuff

It's kind of crazy. I was so opposed to believing that I had a great body.
1. I couldn't see that I had anything close to a great body.
2. I thought it was helpful to hate my body so that I would get up and kick some ass to go change it.
3. I really, really believed my body was gross.

Believing those thoughts did help me take action. But they also made sure I binge-ate at night so I didn't see any results. They kept me stuck in a body and mind I couldn't stand. The most important thing I learned was that these sentences (and the many more terrible things I thought about myself) were what was KEEPING me from making the progress I wanted to make. Knowing that changed my life.

Let's go back to the think → feel → act cycle.

Think: My body is gross

Feel: Upset

Act: Obsess over diets and then eat to feel better

Hating your body will NEVER lead to a positive result. Even sometimes when it seems like it helps us make a change, because it's creating a negative feeling in our body, it is not creating actions that are long-term beneficial, positive, or sustainable.

Out of all of the people I've coached about their relationship with food (a lot), I've never found that these negative thoughts about ourselves produce a positive action and result in our life. It just doesn't happen. Once I knew that to be true, I knew I had to start changing my thinking.

What I had been doing for years just wasn't working. Beating yourself up is OPTIONAL. It doesn't help. Ever. It's not working. Try something new. Like anything else, it's not going to work overnight. It's all about practicing little things every. single. day.

1. Practice intentionally talking to yourself in a kind way.
I like to do this at the gym when it's easier for me to talk to myself in a kind way. Find circumstances that help you be kind to yourself. I feel like a badass at the gym or when I'm all dressed up. Put yourself in situations that help you speak kindly to yourself. Make sure the way you talk to yourself is believable and doesn't make you feel bad. Even a neutral feeling is better than a bad feeling. For example, instead of telling yourself that you hate your thighs, just tell yourself these are my human thighs. They are just thighs. That's it, conversation over. Once you can look at your thighs and not say mean things about them and just notice that they are in fact human thighs, THEN and only then can you start to shift into kindness. The key is believable kindness. My

thighs are strong. My thighs help me walk every single day and that's pretty cool. Not everyone can walk everyday. My thighs are soft. My thighs look good in these jeans. My thighs are kind of sexy. As you can believe more and more kind things about yourself, your beliefs will get better and better. Keep practicing, and take those baby steps. They will add up.

2. If what you're doing isn't working, change it.

I was skeptical. I couldn't understand how loving my body now was going to get me to be really skinny so I could have all of the benefits of being skinny... you know like happiness and more money and a better relationship and self—confidence. But I also knew that what I had been doing for so long wasn't working. I didn't have a body I loved. I talked so much shit about myself in my mind. I was obsessed with thinking about food and what I had already eaten and what I was going to eat and what crazy diet I should try so that I could actually lose weight. I just wanted to know what the hell I needed to do to get skinny, not how to love myself. Something had to change.

So as you're reading, just consider, what if I'm right about this? What if I know you a little better than it seems? What if this was the thing that truly changed everything for you? It can be super scary to change, but I need you to let yourself be open to this.

Here's something I really want you to ask yourself. What do you think you will *feel* when you have what you are picturing as the most amazing, extraordinary body? I thought I would feel confident, proud, happy, connected, motivated, rich, joyful, and on and on and on. So I created an extraordinary body and I didn't really feel any of those things for long. And I definitely didn't feel them for any longer than how often I felt them before I had the body I always wanted.

I realized that I had to work on feeling better instead of trying to change my appearance in order to try to feel better. Things don't make you feel better. You make you feel better. Let me say that again. Things don't make you feel better. *You* make you feel better.

I had to create the feelings of confident, proud, happy, connected, motivated, rich, and joyful myself. No one and nothing was going to give those things to me, not even an incredible body. I had to create them. So if what you're doing isn't working, it's time to make a change.

3. Consider that you just might have an extraordinary body right now.

Bodies are crazy. Honestly, the more I think about it, the more it blows my mind. Bodies just grow out of seemingly nowhere. And then they work all by themselves for almost 100 years. They just know exactly what to do and how to work well. Bodies can do insane things like run hundreds of miles without stopping. They can birth other humans. They can heal from terrible injuries.

- What if you started to believe your body was extraordinary right now? Your mind might find a lot of reasons why that's true: My body is extraordinary because it knows to store fat in places like around my uterus to protect all of my future babies.
- My body is extraordinary because it keeps all of the extra calories I consume as fat so that I could survive longer without needing food.

- My body is extraordinary because it can lift super heavy things and run super far.

It's extraordinary. It's beautiful. It's so damn incredible. What if yours is too? Right now. As it is.

Exercise: Baby Steps to Loving Your Extraordinary Body

1. What do you think about your body currently? How it looks? How it feels? How you wish it would be different?

2. Now imagine I had a magic wand and could change your body immediately into the exact body you want. Picture it.

3. Write all of the things that would come to mind if you had that body. What would you think about it? How would it feel?

4. How does it feel to think all of those things about this perfect body?

5. What would you do to take care of yourself if you felt that way in your new body? Would you buy new clothes to dress it in a way that feels good? Would you make it a priority and take care of it and make sure to make decisions to keep your body feeling good? Get specific. What are all of the things you would do?

6. Correct me if I'm wrong here, but you're saying you would take even BETTER care of your body if you thought really nice things about it? What's stopping you from thinking those really nice things now?

7. Practice intentionally talking to yourself in a kind way. If when you talk to yourself in a kind way, your mind replies "yeah right," take a smaller step towards kindness until you get closer and closer to believing the things you want to believe about your body. "These are my human thighs." "My thighs are strong." "My thighs help me walk every single day and that's pretty cool." "Not everyone can walk everyday." "My thighs are soft." "My thighs look good in these jeans."

Love the Process

"Those who are certain of the outcome can afford to wait, and wait without anxiety." —Gabrielle Bernstein

While I 100% believe we should love our bodies right now, I'm still so damn in for you choosing to love where you're at AND wanting to change. Just because you want to, because it would be kinda fun, or because you want to prove to yourself you can do hard things. This is going to be a process of change. It's uncomfortable, and it is going to last a while, maybe even your entire life.

If this is you, please learn from my mistakes. Love the process of change instead of doing things you can't stand doing because you think it's necessary to create what you want. It's not. Create the body you want in a way that you love.

The bad news is you're not going to be able to create a process that you'll 100% love 100% of the time. Our minds are always going to create conflict and resistance, but you can get pretty close. You can create a process that you enjoy the vast majority of the time. This process to create the body you want and also to become the person you want is a never ending one. You're never going to arrive and then be able to stop. It's an everyday journey without a finish line. Which can feel pretty defeating if you're expecting to get to the finish line so you can feel better.

In the past, I did so many things I hated to try to feel better. I was literally creating the opposite of what I wanted. I was eating things I didn't like. I was working out in ways I didn't like. I was spending my time in ways I didn't like. And I sure as hell was thinking in a way I didn't like. I didn't think it was possible for me to actually enjoy the way I ate, moved my body, and looked. I didn't believe I could have it all. But you can. I can. We ALL can. We can have it all.

I love to believe that I get to have it all. I made it true. I really do have it all. And the way to get there is to start doing the things you enjoy now. It is finding the ways to create the body you want that you could sustain forever and really enjoy.

A few of my favorite ways to love the process is the way I choose to move my body. I love using my Apple watch to track at least 30 minutes of movement per day. It's not always a crazy workout, sometimes it's just walking or stretching. But I do things I love and want to do forever. My favorite gym, The 12, (it's located in Orange County, CA and you definitely need to come try it out) is a place that I absolutely love to workout. Honestly my gym time is often the highlight of my day. The community there is incredible, the workouts make me feel like a badass, and I never leave without words of encouragement and smiles. It helps me exercise in a way that I love. I also love to go for walks with my puppy, Wilder. I love using Classpass to try all kinds of different workout classes like kickboxing and ballet. I love to roller skate. I love practicing handstands. I love emkfit's workout dance Youtube videos. And I even love some line dancing. Oh, and yes I really actually do enjoy running half marathons (which is something I never thought I'd ever say.

I no longer do fasted cardio every day of the week. I no longer spend almost three hours at a time in the gym. I no longer do boring workouts that I hate. It's just simply not a thing I'm willing to do.

I feel the same way about the food I consume. I used to eat and drink things I absolutely hated so that I could be skinnier. I drank plain matcha powder with hot water (maybe some people like this, but I hated it), I would drink straight shots of apple cider vinegar, and mix cayenne pepper into my water. I did it not because I enjoyed any of them at all, but just because I wanted to be skinnier. I am no longer willing to do that. Now I'm not afraid to eat bagels, candy, pizza, or pasta. There's really nothing I won't eat now. But I have full control over my eating now and don't binge on anything. I stop eating when I'm satisfied, and I occasionally track my food to make sure I'm eating the right amount of food and am getting enough protein in.

The rules are all made up. You can literally eat all kinds of foods and have the body you want. Let the rule book in your head go and create what you enjoy and what works for you.

You also have to love the process about the thoughts you practice thinking about yourself. I no longer tolerate terrible thoughts about myself. I know they're useless and just keep creating things I don't want. I practice all kinds of different ways to keep my mind sharp. I'm always reading and listening to new books to learn more about myself and love experimenting with their suggestions for how to get better. You are in charge. Only allow in things you love. Love the process. All of it.

Exercise: Create The Process You Enjoy

1. What workouts do you enjoy doing? List as many as you can think of.

2. What healthy foods do you love eating? How can you make eating healthy easier and more enjoyable? What would your ideal diet look like? Carbs and cookies are all allowed.

3. How would you like to keep your mental health improving in a way you enjoy?

Chapter 4: Create Extraordinary Relationships

"You're not lost, you're just early in the process." —Gary Vaynerchuk

I vividly remember when my biggest life concern was that I believed my family was cursed. I was afraid I would never get married, not because I didn't want to, but because I thought I would never find someone I wanted to marry and who wanted to marry me. I didn't know anyone with a healthy romantic relationship. My mom was always single or in a short-term relationship with some guy that ended up being a D-bag. My aunt was a single mom too and was never married. My grandparents were married, but had the kind of marriage I basically wanted the opposite of. All around me I saw single women or shitty relationships. I didn't want that for me. So I decided to create the opposite, and I'm so proud of how far I've come. Here are my stories and epiphanies about relationships, and I hope they help you create the extraordinary relationships in your life that you deserve.

The Relationship Manual

"I think marriage vows need a rebranding. Instead of "I promise to love you forever", it should be "I promise to be accountable and not blame you or try to change you. I promise to make my emotional health my priority. And I promise to show up even when I'm not in the mood."
—Jillian Turecki

As humans with human brains, we all have manuals for how other people should behave. We all have one for our mother, our partner, our friends, and literally every other human. Your manual might have rules like "They should listen to me when I'm talking." "They should put equal effort in." "They shouldn't say that." "They should help out." This list goes on and on. And the crazy thing is we usually never tell that person that we have these rules for them. We have expectations and guidelines for what other people should do, yet they don't even know that's what we want.

Your manual for your partner might look something like this:
You should compliment me more. You should help with the kids more. You should support me in my diet. You should take out the garbage when it's full. You should drink less. You should want to have sex more often. You should be home more often. You should work less. You shouldn't look at other women or like their selfies on Instagram. You should be more romantic. You should call me more.

These manuals are the cause of our suffering. These manuals create pain and conflict. These manuals are the one thing that stop us from having extraordinary relationships.

We want people to behave differently so that we can feel better. I want him to compliment me more so I feel more confident. I want him to help with the kids more so I feel less stressed and upset. I want him to support my diet so I feel more at ease and motivated.

We give people in our lives way too much power. We incorrectly think that their actions impact our feelings. While sometimes it absolutely feels like the people we love impact our feelings, there is always another stop in between that we are completely in charge of. Our thoughts. They do something, we think something, and THEN we feel. I always joke with my partner and say "You exist, and I feel annoyed." He can't make me feel annoyed, my thoughts make me feel annoyed. But I just have to joke and remind him that he exists and I'm annoyed simultaneously. It's never his fault (even though it feels like it's absolutely his fault).

So... if we have manuals because we want to feel better, and people following or not following our manuals actually don't create our feelings, how do we feel better? You have to change the way you're thinking. Do you ever notice how the same thing can happen in different scenarios and you can feel totally different? My partner can say the same sentence to me on two different days, and on one day I laugh, and on the other day I'm angry. The sentence was the same, but my thoughts about it were different. How do you want to think and feel around your partner (or mother or friend)? Start practicing those thoughts and feelings on purpose, even if they don't follow the manual you have for them.

Notice what the unspoken and completely made up rule book says about everyone in your life. Decide if you want to keep these expectations. Decide if you want to tell the people in your life what you want from them instead of just secretly expecting.

You can ask them to do what you want them to do, but don't put your emotions on the line. Whether they choose to complete your request or not, you've got your own back and you can still feel good. Their action or inaction can not dictate your happiness. Stop expecting people to be who you want them to be or to be different from who they are. Focus on how you want to show up.

I suggest you throw away your manual and let the people in your life be who they are, even when the actions they are taking are not what you think they should be doing. You can feel better regardless. It can be hard to let people be who they are. You can always share your wants, needs, and hopes. You can ask them to change, invite them to do things differently, and try to help them. But ultimately they are going to be who they want to be.

Let me give you a real life example. It has been almost a full week since I asked my partner to sweep off the deck outside. He said he would do it last week. It's still not done and I have a feeling it's not going to be done unless I do it. And that's totally fine. In the past, this would not have been totally fine. I could have easily let myself get upset about it, think he should act differently, ask him 10 more times, stop doing the other things I do around the house, get passive aggressive, etc. But I get to decide: do I want to sweep the deck or do I want to be ok with the deck being dirty? If I want it to be clean that badly, I can do it. No big deal. He thinks it's cold outside and we're not using the deck anyways so who cares. So I chose to just be fine with a dirty deck for now. I asked for what I wanted from him and then left it up to him. I didn't base my emotions on what he chose to do and dropped my manual for how I think he should behave. I decided that this wasn't actually a big deal and by thinking it would probably do more harm than good. (Update: he did eventually sweep the deck.)

Wanting the people in your to be someone different is hurting you. They get to be who they are. You get to decide what to think and feel about it. You can choose to love them unconditionally.

This doesn't mean that you shouldn't have boundaries and you shouldn't leave when necessary. This of course does not apply to any kind of abuse. Some things you will have in your manual and will want to keep in your manual, like they should respect me and be honest with me. Those are non—negotiables. If you are in any kind of relationship that includes abuse, disrespect, or dishonesty, you should leave that relationship. However you are not required to feel hate or anger doing it.

Exercise: What to Do with Your Manual

1. Write down 10 things that are in your manual for a particular person in your life. It can be anyone from a friend, to your partner, to your mom.
2. How would you think and feel if they followed your manual for them perfectly?
3. Notice that you can think and feel that way even if they don't follow that manual.
4. Write down everything you don't like about this person. Don't be afraid to say all of the ugly things. Don't hold back or edit yourself.
5. Go back through your list and notice how many of the things you said about that person are true about yourself, too. Many of our

judgments about others are projections of judgments we have about ourselves. This will increase your awareness.

6. Have you told this person that you think they should do the unspoken things in your manual for them? Brainstorm how to have a productive conversation about how to tell this person what you want.

I feel [emotion] when you work until 9pm because the story in my head says [reason]. I want [your wants]. Would you please [request].

For example: I feel sad when you work until 9 pm because the story in my head says you don't care about me. I want special time for just the two of us in the evenings. Would you please consider coming home early a few nights so we can spend that time together?

Relationship Beliefs

"If we could change ourselves, the tendencies in the world would also change." —Mahatma Gandhi

"Choose love always." This is the advice I give. It's such a well-intentioned statement. It's easy to say, but it takes practice to live it out. I used to have a mental dialogue that often included things like: "I hate everyone." "People suck."

Those were the mottos I lived by back in high school. I remember it being cool to just hate everyone we knew except for our small group of friends. And beyond just hating everyone, men especially had a very negative space in my head.

"Never trust a man." "Men are shit." That's what I was told. "They only want one thing." I heard that so many times. And I believed it. I was terrified that I would never get married. I thought good men just didn't really exist and that I would end up like the vast majority of the women in my family–either never married, or in a relationship they hated but wouldn't leave.

I decided at around 20-years-old that one day I would just get artificially inseminated and become a single mom like the women in my family closest to me. I thought it would be easier so I wouldn't have to deal with any "men bullshit."

I remember saying when I was younger that our family was cursed. No one could find a good man. And now I understand the curse is actually our belief system–the belief that women are better, that men are bad, that it's easier and better to just be alone. Those beliefs about men and relationships were the beliefs that were going to curse me.

Those were the things that I needed to change in order for me to find a man and have the relationship I truly wanted. I had to change the way I talked and thought about men, about relationships, about people, and about myself. I had to be willing to consider that life in a long—term relationship could be easier than being alone. I had to look at all of the amazing men around me and see that men are actually such great people.

There were many steps in between. I couldn't just decide one day I wanted a whole new set of beliefs. There was a lot of history and even subconscious thoughts going on that needed to be changed. It took time and practice to intentionally choose what I wanted to believe and practice that. I had to find evidence of those new beliefs being true so that I could really, truly believe it. And all of the work was worth it.

People who believe men are trash will most likely end up in trash relationships. I committed to creating something different.

And the most important part is that it can end with you. Beliefs as well as traumas can be passed down generation after generation. They will be passed down if **you** don't look at them and heal them. You are not your family. You have the power to start something new. It's not a family curse. You can change it.

Exercise: Creating New Beliefs

1. What are your current relationship beliefs? Write for as long as possible to get absolutely everything out. Create the awareness of what your current mind is believing.

2. Look at your list of beliefs and determine which ones you want to keep and which ones you'd like to throw away forever. It may be helpful to cross out any you don't want anymore.

3. Prove yourself wrong. Write about if there has ever been a time when your current belief hasn't been true. Notice that your brain will mostly remember things that go along with your current belief system.

4. Decide what you would believe if you could truly believe anything. The sky is the limit. Write it down.

5. Practice your new beliefs slowly and with compassion for yourself. Take baby steps. What feels a little better than your current belief that's a little closer to the new belief you want? Make sure you actually believe it or else your very smart brain will call BS.

6. Write down every time something happens according to your new belief.

7. Bonus: Try therapy to uncover unconscious relationship beliefs you may not even know you have.

Example:
Current belief — I hate men.
Belief I want — Men are amazing.
Practice — There are men out there that are amazing. (Believable and closer to the new belief you want.)

Find — Take note of EVERY time you notice a man that does something amazing.

Example:
Current belief — There's no way I'll be able to make $100k per year.
Belief I want — It's easy for me to make $100k.
Practice — I'm willing to keep trying and do whatever it takes to figure out how to make $100k in a 12 month time period, and one day it might even be easy.
Find — Take note of every time making money is easy.

You won't be able to believe new things overnight. It will take time and practice. Journal about it daily. Write it on a sticky note. Set an alarm so your new belief will pop up on your phone throughout the day. Keep practicing and you'll be believing new things in no time.

Daddy (and Family) Issues

"Just because the past didn't turn out like you wanted it to, doesn't mean the future can't be better than you ever imagined."
—Ziad K. Abdelnour

Oh, don't we all have them. I hope you don't, but we all have our story. This is mine. It's one of my favorite stories even though if you had told me that back when I was 13, I never would have believed you. I thought that part of my life sucked. Little did I know, it was working out in the best way.

I have to start way back in the beginning with my mom. She was 21, had just moved to San Diego for college, and met a cute southern boy who called her ma'am and carried her laundry. I mean, I can't blame my mom...ew... but, you know, I get it. So from what I understand, they were kind of dating but it wasn't anything serious. My mom will still insist it was an immaculate conception, but she will also insist that I never drink with boys in a hot tub, so I have some idea of how I came into being.

My mom was 21 and got pregnant. My dad offered to marry her and she said uh, no way, Jose. I don't even love you. Maybe not exactly those words, but that's how I picture it. And then my mom told my dad something along the lines of "I've got this. Leave us alone please and thank you." My mom grew up with my grandparents getting divorced and has every bad divorce story in the books. She hated growing up like that and she didn't want that for me.

So my mom was a freaking champion and had me all on her own at 22. She finished school, worked, and somehow maintained a rockin' bod while doing all of it.

My grandpa was also there to help. He took me to all of the father-daughter dances for Girl Scouts and braided my hair and took me to the most fun places after school. Throughout my childhood, my dad respected my mom's wishes and left us alone.

I also remember being pissed as a kid. On Father's Day, I would really get upset about not having a dad. I would fill out the Father's Day papers that included things like "I love my dad because..." with really sarcastic, angry comments. I really wanted a little brother, too.

My mom explained why I didn't have a dad in my life, but she didn't want to give me his name and contact information because I was still too young and she was afraid he would try to get custody, I would have to live with him over the summer, would hate it, and there would be nothing we would be able to do about it.

Finally when I was 15, I asked for his information for the 100th time and she said okay. I totally didn't expect that one. I didn't know what to do or say or if I really even wanted to call him. My mom had me fully prepared for him to say, "I don't have a daughter. Never call this number again."

I waited until Father's Day to call. I called, and no one picked up. I left a message and said "Hi, This is Felicia. Call me when you get this. Happy Father's Day." What. A. Message.

About a week later, I got a call on my flip phone. "Hi," I said. My dad said "Hi, is this Debbie?" (My mom.) "No, this is Felicia." Silence. Silence for a loooong time. And then I handed the phone to my mom. They talked first for about an hour and then my dad talked to me. He told me all about his life in Louisiana. His wife. His son. His parents. All of which had no idea I existed. We started talking a lot after that and my mom and I made plans to meet him in about six months.

My mom and I flew down to Louisiana to meet them around Christmas time. I remember feeling like jello on that plane. I remember thinking,

"You're not supposed to meet your dad. You're supposed to know him." Everyone was at the airport. My dad, step-mom, little brother, step-brother, and grandpa. Meeting them for the first time felt totally natural. It wasn't weird or awkward. It was like being home.

My mom and I spent the weekend there. I was so in love with my little brother, Ethan. I had always wanted a little brother. I had one without even knowing it. It worked out perfectly.

We had just planned to stay in Louisiana for a weekend, and when our flight got delayed one full day, I was so happy. I remember falling asleep my last night there on the couch, crying. Crying with gratitude and amazement and wanting to stay forever. I couldn't have had a happier ending.

My step-mom is the greatest ever. It doesn't feel like she's a step-parent and we get along like best friends. She easily could have divorced my dad because of this. She had no idea her husband had a child. But she chose to do the thing that was most beneficial for us, for me. And she loves me like a mom does.

My dad is the most amazing and hard—working man ever. He gives me the best dad life advice ever. He treats me like a princess. He's the dad I'd always wanted.

My little brother, Ethan, is my favorite person ever. Last time after I visited him, I sent a quick text to let him know I had an awesome time with him, and he called me and told me how thankful he is for me. He said he was scared when they told him he had a sister, and that he's so glad it was me. He gives better compliments than any other boy, and he is the sweetest and smartest kid ever. You just have to brag a little sometimes, ya know?

Sometimes it looks like there will be daddy issues for life and no possibility of a happy ending. Sometimes you have no idea that your happily ever after is right around the corner. Sometimes a shitty past makes you think you're destined for a shitty future. Sometimes a shitty past is exactly what was necessary to create the most extraordinary future. You decide.

Exercise: When Bad Creates Good

1. Think of a time (or times) in your life when in the moment, it seemed so bad. But in the end, it ended up being a good thing.

2. Remember these moments when things get hard. Many times the bad brings us so much good. Goodness is coming. You've got this.

What Did I Do to Deserve You?

"You are the average of the five people you spend the most time with."
—Jim Rohn

This well-known quote explains that you will become like the people you are around. But what's missing is that all the people your friends are around will also influence you. Studies have shown that the habits of your friend's friends will impact you, even if you don't know those people (so people you've never even met have an impact on you!!).

My boyfriend's roommate knows some amazing ways to eat really healthy while still eating food that tastes amazing. He eats healthy yogurt, frozen berries, granola, and sugar—free syrup before bed. My boyfriend started to eat it often. Then I started to eat it often too. His habit spread to both of us, and I have no doubt the habit will keep spreading to people who know me. Some habits have a 45% likelihood of spreading to friends. This is how important it is to choose who you spend time with wisely.

I truly have the most incredible people in my life, amazing friends, and community, and people who help me create amazing new habits, while kicking the ones I don't want.

So if we pick up habits from friends, and friends of friends, the key is attracting and finding the friends who will bring more of what you want in your life. If you want to up-level your business, go to business events where you're the least successful person in the room. If you want to be more cultured, find and spend time with people who love theater or museums. If you want to become a better employee, spend time with the high achievers, even if it's uncomfortable. If you want to learn more about how to help the planet, go to groups where people are doing just that. And be willing to stop spending so much time with people who have habits and qualities that you don't want for yourself.

Be the kind of person you want to be around. Be amazing if you want to have amazing people in your life. Be a good human. Spend time with people you want to be more like. Love often and love hard.

Exercise: Attracting Amazing Humans

1. Describe the kind of best friend you want in your life. Add every amazing quality and cool thing they would do that would make them the best friend ever.

2. Identify the things from that list you can start doing or acting on in your own life.

3. This week, commit to making a connection with one new person you want in your life. Don't be creepy and weird about it. Make a connection over something you have in common and ask to do something with them that is valuable to both of you. Do not ask someone to have coffee and "pick their brain" because this will not be of value to them. Instead find something that will be fun and interesting for both of you. This will be an uncomfortable exercise for you to do. Do it anyway. You'll be better because of it.

Don't Have Sex

"If you obey all of the rules, you miss all of the fun."
—Katharine Hepburn

"You did it!!" I told myself. You had sex and you don't feel unbearable amounts of shame!!! I was so proud of myself. I had casual sex with someone and nothing bad happened. AND I didn't hate myself.

Growing up, all I ever heard was "Don't have sex! You'll get pregnant and die." (Well, that's basically what it felt like they were saying at least.)

I got really involved in church in middle school, not because my family was really into church, but because my home life felt really hard and the church people were the most kind, loving, welcoming, and fun people I had ever met and all I wanted was to be surrounded by them. Lots of time at church meant I knew damn well that I definitely should never have sex until I was married. It was ingrained in me.

I didn't know many people who were having sex in high school. Yes, maybe I wasn't a super cool kid; I realize that now. I started wearing a purity ring at around 16 years old with the intention to save myself for marriage. I didn't want to lose my virginity to just anyone. I decided that it needed to be ideally with my husband, but if not, with someone super special.

So as my #foreveralone life went on, there wasn't any sign of a serious relationship in sight. Yes, there were hookups and times I reallllly wanted to have sex with some hot, hilarious guy with an accent I met while traveling, but I kept that commitment to myself that I wanted it to be ~serious~ when I decided to lose my virginity. Also, if I ever told anyone I was a virgin, they didn't want much to do with me, LOL.

When I was 23, I got into my first serious relationship. I moved to New Zealand for a year and met a guy on Bumble and fell in love. Once we were in a committed relationship for a while, I decided I was ready to lose my virginity (and not just ready, but like dying to). And I'll just fast forward here; we had sex, but we eventually broke up. Immediately after we broke up, I was thinking how I wanted to get out there and have that mindblowing casual sex everyone talked about. I felt like I still hadn't experienced that.

I wanted to have my ho phase and now that I wasn't a virgin anymore it seemed like less of a big deal. I wanted to go get 'em, tiger.

I didn't have sex for a year and a half after my breakup. There was really just no one I wanted to have sex with. All of the guys I was going on dates with just kinda sucked. They just seemed boring and there wasn't any chemistry. It was totally the opposite of what I thought would happen.

On the first date I went on after the breakup, I cried. (I thought that was just a thing that happens in movies—crying on dates, crying during/after sex, becoming a psycho, etc.) No, no. That's real life. The guy just seemed a little crazy (long story short: he told me stories about his neighbors calling the cops on him multiple times) and I missed my ex-boyfriend.

The vast majority of my friends told me sex outside of a relationship wasn't great at all. Some of my friends saved sex until marriage. I still felt like sex was a big deal and something to be very careful with.

I decided to actively work on changing those beliefs, not because I think the ho life is the way to go, but because I personally decided that for me, I didn't want to be ashamed if I wanted to have casual sex. That's what I chose when I thought about "what I would choose if it was amazing either way?"

Maybe my decision to become less ashamed of sex started when I really reconsidered what I believed religion-wise in when I lived in Rishikesh, India for a month. I saw how dedicated the people I met were to their religion. My Bollywood dance teacher would do entire day-long fasts often to become closer to God. My yoga teachers based their life around religion. The Indian people were the most welcoming and kind people I had met.

The Christian religion had taught me that they wouldn't get into heaven because they didn't believe in Jesus. A bunch of privileged Americans would all get into heaven, but the people in India—they didn't believe in Jesus, so heaven was definitely not where they were going. That just didn't make any sense to me.

The more I traveled, the more people I met who were incredible people yet they didn't believe in Jesus. And then I found out that my college-group pastor, who very much ingrained in us that whatever we do, we better not have sex, was sexting girls in the college group asking them what their favorite sex position was. Oh, and he was also married with kids.

My thinking had been flawed. I couldn't trust in the Christian religion like I so blindly had before. I just did not believe that all of the amazing non-Jesus people I met were going to hell and all of the shitty Jesus people I met were going to heaven.

There had to be more than this. I believe there is a God. I believe that all humans should guard their hearts and not just give their bodies away in order to find love. I believe everything I went through as a Christian happened to help me. I met so many amazing people by becoming a part of the Christian community.

But then I decided I didn't want to be a part of it anymore. I wanted to take in everything I had learned and decide what being an amazing person meant to me. I decided that I could still be an amazing person (and wife) if I wanted to have sex for fun.

Even though I distanced myself from the religion that had been such a huge part of my life for so long, I still wasn't having sex. I still wasn't meeting people I had that connection with. I was still nervous that if I slept with someone, I would feel so much shame.

And finally a year and a half after my one and only relationship, I met someone on Bumble (yes, another Bumble winner) and actually kinda liked him. He made me dinner with fish he had caught that day with home-made mashed potatoes that were even dairy-free because I'm a princess. He was cute, fun, and the connection was there.

We had sex. The most terrible sex I've ever had. But we had sex. And I didn't feel bad about it.

I didn't let myself believe I was less of a classy woman or future—wife. I didn't let myself believe God would be mad at me for it. I didn't let myself believe I was doing a bad thing. I just chose to decide on purpose how I wanted to think about casual sex. And it was pretty damn fun.

I was so thankful I had questioned those beliefs I had for so long. It was a HUGE step for me. I knew this was a belief I wanted to change because I was so curious about it, and I thought about it a lot. I felt shame and guilt when I thought about changing it, but also curiosity and a desire to try things differently. That's how I decided it was a belief I wanted to question and change.

It worked out well for me, but if I had tried it and then decided it was a terrible idea and I didn't enjoy it, I would have gone back to what I had always done AND would have chosen to love myself for trying. I was willing to feel courageous. It's HARD to do something you've always been told is bad. I had the courage (courage usually feels super uncomfortable by the way) to try something different, to go against what I was always taught, and to give myself some space to try things differently to see if they fit without judging myself.

My belief about sex was such a deep belief, but I knew if I kept trying I could change it. I had to do the belief work in my mind, but also get out there, take action differently from how I always had, and choose that no matter what I would love myself the whole way through. Each stage of life is so valuable and we only get to live it once. You have to create it on purpose, question everything, and have so much fun along the way.

Exercise: What You Believe & Why You Believe It

1. Write out all of the beliefs you have about one part of your life that you want to change. (Examples: beliefs about sex before marriage, beliefs about what kind of career you could have, beliefs about how much money you could make, beliefs about the kind of relationship you have with your partner or mother)

2. Where did those beliefs come from? Why do you believe them?

3. Imagine there are no rules. You won't damage your soul by being intimate with people. You won't get fat from eating carbs. You don't need social media to run a successful business. What beliefs would you choose to keep, and which would you change? You are actively creating your life and reality and you do get to decide what you can create. Choose carefully and dream big.

4. Find evidence of how your existing beliefs are not true. (Example: I believe sex before marriage is bad, but I do have a few friends who completely recommend it, so it could be possible I'm wrong about this.)

5. Go back to the Relationship Beliefs section and do the work to change your beliefs to ones that will help you create an extraordinary life.

Best Breakup Ever

"The past doesn't exist except as a memory, a mental story, and though past events aren't changeable, your stories about them are."
—Martha Beck

There was no way I felt like I could just break up with him. Nothing bad even happened. I loved him too much. He was my first love, my first everything. He was the first guy that I didn't think was horrible.

I was raised in a family of strong, independent women who were not afraid to say that men are shit, and that's what I was raised to believe. Everything around me proved it to be true. It's funny, when you have a belief about something, your brain just keeps looking for evidence of it in the world over and over to make the belief even more believable. I found evidence everywhere.

I've mentioned that my mom was never married. Her boyfriends were in and out as I grew up. My grandparents had both been married and divorced multiple times. My cousin's dad had been in jail. I didn't grow up with my dad and probably would have never met him if I never took the initiative to find him. I had a pretty crappy view of men in general.

I went through stages of being absolutely terrified that I would end up like my family, never be in a great relationship, and be lonely and miserable, and stages of being completely confident I would be happy if I was alone and adopted all the children and didn't have to take anyone else's shit.

Then I decided to move across the world all by myself because...well because why not? I was young and that's the time to go explore, right?! I figured that once I had a big girl job and a family of my own, I wouldn't be able to just pick up and move.

It actually all started when I was in a dirty hostel in Cambodia and got a message from a family in New Zealand who saw my ad looking for an au pair job. An au pair is like a nanny that lives with a family in another country and basically exchanges nannying work for food and housing. Most people use an agency to make sure that their future family won't kill them or screw them over, but that sounded more complicated and less ~spontaneous~. So I posted an ad, looking for a family that would let me live with and work for them in Australia or New Zealand, and I had tons of replies, but there was one family who kept messaging me.

At my dirty Cambodian hostel, the night after a pub crawl, I FaceTimed a family who I actually couldn't even understand 72% of the time because of hostel wifi and their accents. Regardless, I committed on the spot to move in with them for a full year. It was such an adrenaline rush. Making travel plans was for sure my drug of choice.

Before I left to begin the job, everyone and their mother was telling me that I would go to New Zealand and fall in love and never come back. I said, "No, no, no. That would be horrible and I'd rather not." But of course, that was for sure secretly at the top of my to-do list.

Just for some background, my relationships so far had looked like this:

A three-month boyfriend in high school who I didn't really even like but he was friends with my friends and he was really nice to me, so I figured why not.

Then a hot firefighter who taught me how to dance and whom my 18-year-old self wanted to marry, but then he broke up with me after a week and three days because we lived an hour apart and that was too far. Yes, it was exactly a week and three days. I can't forget.

And then there was the guy who would have been my choice when answering the question "if you could use a love potion on anyone, who would it be?" He was the guy that every girl I knew had a crush on. Awesome family. Really, really good looking. Kind. The perfect Christian. He was it. And I worked my butt off to get into his inner circle. Then we became best friends. But we were the kind of best friends that did super date-y stuff, but nothing romantic, which made it an even closer relationship. Of course I was in love with him the whole time, and then he finally told me he liked me, and I went home and woke my mom up and freaked out like an 11-year-old girl because I was so excited. Then a couple weeks later he texted me and said, "Hey, just want to make sure you know we're just friends." Ah, yeah, totes. Now he's married. Life is weird. Okay, back to my story. New Zealand.

The first thing I did when I got there was get on Bumble. I remember sitting in my new room with all of my suitcases still full and getting on Bumble. I was so excited. I went on a few dates. One guy was super boring and I couldn't wait to leave. Another guy was pretty cool, but then unmatched me as soon as we left the date. LOL.

And then there was Ryan. You know how when you're swiping and you match with someone who is an actual angel sent from the gods and is super good looking and has a good combination of adventure and non-selfie pictures and a bio that isn't super douchey, and all you can think is well that's nice but they 100% are not going to reply to me, and then you move on? He was that guy...except he actually replied.

I'm kind of a total weirdo because I still remember his bio, and it said "Just looking for someone to watch Netflix and eat peanut butter out of the jar with. Bonus points if you have a pug." I messaged him and said "Hey Ryan, peanut butter is my favorite." (Total giveaway that I was not from New Zealand..."favorite" vs "favourite"...rookie move.) He replied and said "Hey Felicia, I'm about to be your new favorite." I was like dayum, okay who is this guy?! And that's how it all started.

We chatted for about a month. I was obsessed with him before I even met him. I was excited for the evenings because we would message when he was off work. I told all of my friends about him. And I hadn't even met him, or talked to him on the phone or made sure he wasn't a fat 76-year-old man. But there was just something there. He asked me about my goals and what they meant to me. I just knew this guy was different.

So after about a month of talking, we went on our first date. We went ice skating and had frozen coke from Maccas (that's what they call McDonald's). We talked about real life stuff like investments and businesses. I told him about my side hustles and he offered to help me. He was just different from the rest of them. I couldn't tell you why, but I just kept telling myself, "Yep, this is it. This is the guy." I just decided, after meeting him for 15 minutes, he was it.

It was the perfect first date, nothing weird, just fun. The next day we talked. He was lazy and hungover from a concert he had gone to the night before (he invited me, but I had plans already), and I had nothing to do all day. I suggested we do nothing together. So we did. We cuddled and watched *Harry Potter* and got the best waffles ever covered in chocolate and peanut butter and ice cream.

On his birthday two days later, I took the boy I nannied and drove 35 minutes and met Ryan for lunch on his work break. I thought maybe I was being too much too soon, but I just couldn't get enough of the guy. We were basically inseparable for the next year.

He quit his job to study, and was moving 2.5 hours away to live with his parents. I quit my nanny job and moved in with his parents, too. Just the four of us. But it totally worked. I was so thankful to have a family to live with. That year in New Zealand was one of my favorite years of my life.

Ryan and I went on a trip every single weekend. I think I saw every corner of New Zealand. We swam in waterfalls in the rain, went rafting in glow worm caves, and laid in the grass on a cliff looking over the coast. It was everything I had ever wanted. Ryan was everything I had ever wanted.

He was the only guy that had ever changed the way I thought about men. I saw my entire life with him. Things weren't perfect. Sometimes I got upset and felt like he didn't care about me. I was terrified that we would break up. I thought that having my heart broken would be the worst thing in the world. I always thought I loved him more than he loved me and that really scared me.

Social media reminded me that he didn't make me breakfast in bed or surprise me with extravagant dates, but he did always bring me a preworkout to drink before we went to the gym together and he honored the bets he lost by getting me flowers, and he even gave me a massage when I was lucky.

There was really nothing that ever went wrong between us. The only thing that was wrong was the thoughts I was having that maybe it "should" be different. I had never been in another relationship, so I just didn't know. I stayed in New Zealand for a full year. I was much more sad to go back home than I had ever been leaving home.

At that time, I was a little unsure about our relationship because I wasn't sure Ryan had feelings as strong as mine. It was hard for me to tell because we both show love so differently. So I went home. We talked on the phone almost daily and Ryan texted me 'good morning' and 'good night love you x' every day.

We were killin' the long distance thing. Then he booked a ticket to come visit for three weeks. Man, was I happy. Those were by far our best three weeks ever. We went to Vegas and New Orleans and Houston and San Diego and we literally walked to Mexico from California. We stayed in hotels and AirBnbs and Ryan met my entire family. It went so well, like amazingly well. We were so flirty and romantic and it was like we had just fallen in love all over again. We were never on our phones and we spent so much quality time together. It was the best.

Then he left and moved to Melbourne, Australia to live with two of his childhood best friends. He wanted me to wait to come there until he had a job secured. I couldn't wait. I quickly booked a flight to go to Melbourne for three months, with a return date before the holidays.

When I got there, we both were trying to save money and we didn't have a car. I was prepping for my bikini contest and was putting a lot of time and energy into that, and we spent 85% of the time looking at screens.

We're productive people. We like to learn and write and do things, so it's not like we were just doing nothing. But we weren't connecting very much. Ryan still didn't have a job, so I was so happy to have him around all of the time, but the expectations I had after that high of being in the States together meant that it just wasn't the same.

Once he got a job, he was gone for about 12 hours a day at work, and then went to the gym after that. The guy had some serious goals and didn't half-ass anything. Except I guess our relationship was the thing that felt a little half-assed.

We didn't go on dates, wear anything besides gym clothes or pajamas, go on adventures, or leave the house except to get groceries. I was losing it. That was not what I'm used to and it was hard.

I cried almost every day for weeks while I was home alone all day. I tried to meet friends, but I was having a hard time finding anyone I clicked with. I just wanted to spend time with Ryan, and he just wanted to chill alone or with his friends when he wasn't working.

I kept thinking, "He doesn't care about me as much as I care about him." He told me, "In a relationship, one person loves more. And that's you." This freakin' killed me. It absolutely killed me. I thought I deserved better. I thought that was a load of crap.

I was over it. But I also wasn't. I so badly wanted someone to kiss me in the morning and say "good morning" and make time for me and text me a few times during the day and tell me I was pretty every once in a while, especially when I got all dressed up.

I wanted to see if there was someone else out there who would be better for me, but I was terrified that I would never find someone I loved as much as I loved Ryan. I still wanted to be on *The Bachelor* and go live alone in Bali and maybe sleep with more than one person in my whole life. But I wasn't about to let Ryan go.

He encouraged me 110% in all that I wanted to do, no matter how big of a dream it was. He helped make me a better person. He inspired me to set bigger goals.

I was getting job offers back in the States. My job didn't want me full-time because I was in a different time zone. My grandparents were getting sicker. I was really looking forward to going home for the holidays. And I usually never look forward to going home.

I thought a lot about breaking up with Ryan, but if he wanted to be with me really badly, then I wasn't going to let him go. I only wanted to break up because I couldn't tell if he wanted to be with me or not.

The time was getting closer for me to go home. I knew we needed to talk, but I was going to wait until the last day. I just had a feeling.

Our last weekend together was the best. We got massages and kombucha and had a picnic and saw the new *Harry Potter* at the movies and had lots of cuddles. We were pretty dang perfect together when things were good, except neither of us liked doing that whole communication thing. I knew it had to be done. So on our last night, right before we were about to fall asleep, I said we needed to talk. Well, I said I need you to talk. Because I didn't want to. So he just said "hello." See, I told you we were good at this.

After a lot of silence, he talked. He said that we should break up. He said that he wanted me to focus on my career. He said that he knew how happy coaching and helping people makes me. He said he wanted me to do that, and that I would have more opportunities if I stayed back home. He said I should be more selfish and put myself first.

He was right. I wasn't very happy living in Australia. I did have more opportunities at home. I was putting Ryan and our relationship first. I knew ending the relationship needed to be done, but I couldn't have done it. I loved him too much.

We talked about the day we first met and some of our favorite adventures. And we cried. I didn't know I had that many tears in my body. I cried that kind of cry where you make those half-monster, half-dying noises because you can't breathe and everything is drowning in tears and snot. Yeah, that kind.

We said our usual goodnight I love yous and had an extra special cuddle. I think I cried more than I slept that night.

The morning was the same. We cried saying goodbye, not knowing if we would ever see each other again. I went through the day. I cried at the gym like a crazy person. I cried going for a walk. I cried as Ryan's best friend drove me to the airport.

Then his friend said we needed to make a stop. He took me into the supermarket and bought me tissues and two boxes of Tim Tams and six candy bars that we don't have in the States. Maybe that's a little thing, but it meant the world.

How freaking lucky am I? I got to spend some of the best months of my life with Ryan. I got to grow so much and have him in my life. His family let me live with them for months. His best friends loved me and took care of me like I was their best friend. I was going home to a family who loved the heck out of me and was dying to see me.

I was broken up with so that I could go kick ass even more. I was broken up with so that I could be with my family and further my career. I was broken up with so I could find an even better partner that I knew was out there for me.

Best. Breakup. Ever.

Okay, okay. So what does my breakup have to do with you? Let me tell you.

Who in their right mind talks about a breakup being amazing? No one. Because they're generally terrible and sad and especially in my case, full of lots of ugly crying. There is nothing "best ever" about them. Which is why this was super fun for me to write. I wrote this whole chapter on the flight back home from New Zealand in 2018. I MADE this the best breakup ever, and damn did it help me get back to my life and stop obsessing over him.

I decided that immediately after this break up, I got to write the story of it. This is how I wanted to remember it. I could have written a whole sob story about how terrible it all was, how he did it all wrong and how I was all right. But I didn't want that. I didn't want this to be a sad part of my life. Yes, it was sad when I was experiencing it. And I did want to be sad because that relationship was complete. But I wanted this story to be a good one, so I wrote it that way.

I learned that I could change my past. The past only exists in my mind now. I can decide through which lens I look at the situation. Yes, there is value in looking back at the hard parts and learning from them so I don't keep repeating those mistakes again. But for the most part, it wasn't helpful for me to see this as a sad story.

Studies have shown that most of our memories are not completely accurate, and our brain fills in a lot of the gaps. We make things up, even if it's not consciously. Our memories are part factual, and a lot of the story we tell ourselves. So I decided to tell a good story.

I don't say this to tell you to make up fake stories to tell yourself or to gloss over anything negative and make it positive. I do believe our body holds onto traumas we've experienced and sometimes it's not as simple as changing the story you tell. I just want you to be aware that in many instances, you are making up a lot of the story, and you can choose the lens through which you view the story. You might as well make it a good one.

Exercise: Change Your Past
1. Think of a story from your past that is sad or unhappy. Rewrite the story. This time write the story as if you are the hero, not the victim.

What I've Been Waiting For

"You can be a businesswoman, a mother, an artist, and a feminist - whatever you want to be - and still be a sexual being." —Beyonce

"This is what I've been waiting for." That's all I kept thinking that night.

As he took off my clothes at 4 a.m. in the hostel bunk bed, he couldn't stop drooling over me and my body. He was in disbelief that he got to be with me and he let me know it. He made me feel like a goddess. He made me feel so extremely attractive and loved being with me.

He was Kyle. Kyle was the first person I met when I walked into the hostel in Mexico City. I was traveling alone. I was exhausted from traveling all day, but I decided to go check out the hostel terrace before I went to bed in case I met anyone I could hang out with the next day.

While I was used to traveling alone, I always felt better with another person to explore a new city. I noticed Kyle was wearing a wedding ring. He looked young, and typically solo travelers at hostels aren't married. I asked him about it immediately, not necessarily even consciously aware that I was interested in him. I was curious. "Oh. Yeah, no, I'm definitely not married. I was in the Peace Corps in Africa before COVID hit and I wore the wedding ring so people wouldn't try to get me to marry their daughter. I've just kept it on since being home."

Kyle was cool. He was not my type at all. He wasn't strikingly attractive. He was just kinda...a guy. As the days went on, I found myself hoping to see Kyle more and more. He was honestly the only one there that was pretty cool.

Some of the other characters I met at that hostel were:
Evan — a guy who played penny poker online, had lived in Mexico for years, and took new guys at the hostel to the local whorehouse for an exciting first night in Mexico.
Adam — a guy who played guitar (badly, I was told) in the streets of Mexico, had a life mission of spreading the news about anarchy, and

grilled me about why I wore white because that was the kind of unacceptable thing rich people did in his opinion.

Josh — a guy from "Missoura" who raw-dogged a stripper the first night he was there.

Anyway, my point is, Kyle was pretty normal. He was also funny and just super cool.

On the next day, got back to the hostel after a day of solo adventuring and saw Kyle on the terrace again. He asked me to quickly show him one photo of my day out before he and another guy went out for the night. (I was upset that I wasn't invited to their evening plans and considered staying up half of the night to wait for them to get back.) I showed Kyle one photo of the beautiful place I visited that day. You could see a girl in a bikini (me!), small and far away to show how huge and gorgeous the scenery was. I was far away, it was hard to tell it was me in the photo. Kyle quickly looked at the photo and said, "what a cutie." I later found out he didn't even realize that was me in the photo, but of course I was thrilled thinking he was complimenting me.

The next night Kyle asked me to go get tacos. I wasn't hungry, but I wasn't about to pass up an opportunity to spend time with him. He was magnetic. On our way out the door, we ran into another hostel friend, Issac, and our taco date unfortunately ended up with three.

We ate tacos, drank margaritas, hung out at a rooftop bar, and later twerked upside down on the big Mexico City letters in the city center. And then when we went back to the hostel, they wanted to drink some more. So I grabbed a blanket off of my bunk bed and sat outside sipping water until 4 a.m. with them. I'm not a late night person and the idea of doing this sounded terrible to be honest. But this was my chance with Kyle and I wasn't about to go to bed and miss it.

I kept doing little things to try and get his attention. I sat next to him. I tried to touch him at every not weird chance I got. I made my eye contact way more drawn out than I ever have talking to anyone else. I had stopped drinking a long time ago, but I couldn't stop thinking about how I was going to get him in my room.

Finally they decided to call it a night, and Kyle grabbed two of the now three blankets I had brought outside for us all. He brought them into my room. We hugged. We looked each other in the eyes and he said, "See you tomorrow." "Okay, " I replied.

He started walking away. That was the stupidest thing I could have said. Okay?! Literally anything besides okay would have helped me get closer to what I wanted. Okay!!

Thank god the man can read minds because after he took a few steps out the door, he turned his head and looked at me. I was watching his every move. He started walking backwards again towards me. He kissed me.

His kiss took my breath away. It was so thrilling. I was out of breath. I was kissing while trying to inhale any air I could get because I didn't want to stop for just one second to fill my lungs.

We moved to the bed. He touched me gently and whispered in my ear. He slowly undressed me, in awe of me and every inch of my body. Every touch was electric. One thing led to another and he became the third man I let myself become one with.

It was both the most natural and thrilling sex I had ever had. It was that mind-blowing sex everyone had talked about. And I finally got to experience it without guilt or shame. It was just pure pleasure and thrilling fun.

This was it. What I've been waiting for: that mind blowing, casual sex I had been so curious about. I let myself experience it and loved myself through it all. I had changed my belief. This was a huge piece of evidence that I could use to help me create the new belief that casual sex could be incredible. It was a big turning point for me because it was something I had been nervous about for so long. I had successfully changed a huge, deeply rooted belief I had carried for so long and it felt so good.

Keep working on changing beliefs you no longer want. Take action differently. Love yourself through it all.

You're Not My Type

"I hope you don't mind that I put down in words how wonderful life is while you're in the world." —Elton John

Despite the night of hot, casual sex, Kyle wasn't my type. He physically was not my type (he definitely weighs less than I do.) His characteristics (he likes to lay in bed alllll day and isn't goal-oriented) and his values (he never wants to get married or have kids) are literally the opposite of everything I had always looked for.

But he showed me what incredible sex was like for the first time ever. He made me laugh until I almost peed my pants. My favorite moment was when we flew to Cancun together and all of the taxi drivers wanted us to get in their taxi. Kyle put his finger in the no-no finger wag position and started doing a little "no no no" dance for all of the taxi people. Everyone was laughing hysterically and it was my favorite thing ever. He helped me be a little bit sillier and helped me get more comfortable with being uncomfortable in public. He encouraged me to get out of my comfort zone and showed me that it was safe to try new things. He made me feel loved and cared for and he was just super freakin' fun. But still...he wasn't my type. At all.

I let myself like him for a lot of reasons. I was on vacation. It wasn't serious. I wanted a little travel romance. I wanted to explore letting myself have casual sex. It didn't really matter because we were just in Mexico for a short time.

I'm thankful for all of those things because he really helped me relax, stop being a psycho, quit overthinking every person I date, and just have fun. It let me see Kyle for who he really was and love that about him instead of dissecting all of the things that could be bad about him. I was just present and accepting. Little did I know that would change the rest of my life.

Things went really well with Kyle. I unexpectedly started bawling the morning I left Mexico, not knowing if I'd ever see him again and not ready to leave him forever. He left Mexico and came straight to California to spend 10 days with me before going back home to his family in Chicago. We talked for a long time after that and planned to meet up again in the future. (We did end up meeting up again in

California, and then I ended the relationship because I met someone else...more on that coming soon)

It was a wonderful experience all around. I realized that what I had been doing in the past didn't work. Doing the same thing over and over again wasn't going to get me anywhere new. I was always overanalyzing men and finding things wrong with them so I couldn't date them. If I couldn't see myself with them forever after the first date, I turned them down.

I loved to chase men and get the satisfaction of getting them to fall for me. I loved the type of guy that was motivated, had a good job, and cared about investing and preparing for a successful future, a pretty boy who was fit, a guy with a good family and little baggage.

But every time I found him — the guy who checked all of the boxes — it just didn't work out. At all. So after my experience with Kyle, I decided that maybe my type shouldn't really be my type at all anymore. That was a huge lesson for me. Going after my type wasn't working. There is so much more to people, AND there is SO much I can learn by dating people quite the opposite of my type. I became much more open to dating all kinds of men instead of quickly writing them off.

And then I met Levi.

I'm Glad You Love My Dog at First Sight

"No one can fully understand the meaning of love unless he's owned a dog." —Gene Hill

I brought my dog to a wedding. As any crazy dog mom does, I bring him literally everywhere. I put him in a cute little tuxedo and sat him right next to me for the ceremony.

At cocktail hour, I was hanging out with some new and some old friends. There was a guy who absolutely loved my dog. Naturally I love anyone who loves my dog. He just wasn't really my type, so I kept talking to friends and paid little attention to the dog-loving man.

When we found our assigned seats for dinner, I realized I was sitting in between Dog Lover and a couple I knew. I hadn't seen the friend next to me in a while and was so excited to talk to her and her husband about traveling, why everyone I had met traveling did drugs, and what I should do about my job I was considering leaving.

A while later I realized my back was completely turned to Dog Lover for over half of the dinner, which was very rude, so I apologized and kept talking to my friends with my back slightly less turned.

Many margaritas were consumed. We enjoyed dinner and the wedding speeches, and then it was time to dance. I was running around after my dog, making sure he didn't ruin anything and getting some dance time in. Next thing I know, I'm doing the WAP dance on the dance floor with one of my friends. This is something I never ever would have done if I wasn't super drunk and/or I hadn't practiced my WAP-ing in Mexico just earlier that month.

Next thing I know, Dog Lover approached me from behind for some grinding. I remember turning around to look at who was touching me and thinking "eh, sure, whatever." (Levi must have known what my back looked like really well from how much I had it turned to him at dinner.)

It wasn't love at first sight. As it got later and margaritas turned into tequila shots, there was one guy who kept asking for my number and once I told him no, he made sure to let everyone know that I hated him because I wouldn't give him my number. Then there was Levi. He kept asking me to go back to his hotel. He was driving all of his drunk friends back and kept asking me to join. I definitely wasn't going to his hotel because I had a perfectly good van bed 100 feet away with my puppy in it. I wasn't going anywhere.

So I compromised. "You can come back to my van. I'm going to sleep, but I'll leave the door unlocked if you want to come in." I went to bed and fell asleep.

I woke up to Levi coming into my van followed by a nice make out sesh. Cuddles and kissing are basically my love language and I'm happy to just leave it at that. Levi told me all kinds of deep personal details and kept asking me to share some personal stories about my life. He took out a condom, to which I replied, "What kind of girl do you think I am?" So we just cuddled for a while and I fell asleep. That was the night.

Commitment Issues

"Happily ever after is not a fairy tale. It's a choice." —Fawn Weaver

Our love story didn't get much better over the first few months. I was still very unsure about Levi and about dating in general. I had been clear about the fact that I didn't want a boyfriend. I wanted to travel and enjoy more of the casual sex that I had just finally let myself start experiencing. I wanted to enjoy the last few years of my 20s before I got wifed up.

Let me be really honest here. Levi took me on the best dates ever and he was really easy to talk to, so naturally I wanted to keep hanging out with him. He took me to get a fancy 90-minute massage. He took me to restaurants I would never ever pay for myself. He took me to get a facial. He took me (and my dog) to Mammoth Mountain to spend a weekend in the snow. He took me to get a manicure and pedicure. And he always kept me very well—fed.

I had all kinds of thoughts in the beginning that maybe I was doing a bad thing because I wasn't sure about Levi and was enjoying his fun dates. But we were both getting something out of the relationship and I was honest with him that I wanted to travel and not be tied down, so I just enjoyed what it was.

I ended things with him twice. Once in the very beginning, I was still talking to Kyle and had some feelings for him. He was coming to visit me and while nothing was exclusive with either of them, I didn't like talking to two romantic partners at the same time, so I ended things with Levi. He accepted it...but kept talking to me, and after spending more time with Kyle, I decided to end all communication with Kyle and started dating Levi again.

The second time I ended things was after we went to Mammoth for the weekend. I just felt like something was off. I just wasn't as into Levi as I thought I should have been. We were with another seemingly perfect couple all weekend and I felt like my relationship with Levi was seriously lacking. So I ended things again. We stopped talking for a few days, and once again, Levi didn't stop chasing me.

He didn't stop chasing me from day one. This absolutely freaked me out. There were long texts, so long they filled up my entire iPhone screen so you couldn't see what I had said before or after. He was extremely honest and vulnerable with me from the beginning and was eager to hear me share all about who I am and why. He opened up his pretty big pile of baggage and shared it all. He told me that he's a dad. He told me all about his past and some of it was honestly a little scary to hear. And all along, he made it clear that he wanted to be with me.

But because I did what I had always done, I ran away.

When a guy shows a lot of interest in me from the beginning, I always took that as a clear sign that he liked me much more than I liked him, and that things would never work out with uneven levels of liking and so I should end things immediately, which is exactly what I did. But Levi didn't let me. Thank God he didn't, because little did I know, that's exactly what I needed.

We went on dates for months. Some weeks we spent almost every day together. But I still was set on leaving and traveling alone and keeping my commitment issues for as long as possible.

Levi was happy keeping our not-relationship as it was, until the day that he asked me to be his girlfriend. In true Felicia fashion, I freaked out and kept repeating "I don't know". Then Levi said, "Well if you don't know what we are, then I know what we are." I assumed this meant we're officially nothing and it's over.

Then something totally unexpected happened. I had gotten what I wanted — to be nothing, to keep my non-commitment lifestyle, to let him know I was serious about not wanting a boyfriend so I could go live the good life until I was 30 when I would suddenly want to settle down.

I kind of freaked out that I had potentially just let my relationship with Levi go. I didn't expect to truly realize that I did actually want something with Levi. I didn't want to let him go. But the night went on, and we were still officially nothing.

Two days later I made a huge, scary decision. It was the day I was leaving to drive from California to Louisiana alone with no idea when I would come back. It was a trip that was planned for a while already and I knew that if I really did want to end things with Levi, leaving California for a while would probably be an easy way to do it.

But I knew I didn't want to end things with Levi. I simply made the decision that I was ready to be all-in because I knew so strongly that I didn't want this to be over. I told him I would stop to say bye one last time before my trip. I stopped at a Nutrishop on the way to his house and bought all of the protein snacks and energy drinks that I knew Levi would love. I wrote a sweet card. I drove to Levi's, gave him the box of treats, and asked him to be my boyfriend. He hesitated and asked if I was really sure. We both said yes. And then I left on my trip to Louisiana.

From this, I realized that getting exactly what I thought I wanted wasn't what I wanted at all. I stuck to my situation beliefs and knew I was exactly where I was supposed to be and that I would always have my own back, no matter what happened.

I had always been a person that was so anti-commitment that I would literally tape stickers instead of sticking them because once I stuck them, that was a done deal. I got a trial week at every single gym in my area because I didn't want to sign the contract. And I was convinced a boyfriend was the last thing I wanted. Until Levi very nonchalantly basically told me that if I wanted to be nothing, that's what I would get. I was so sure I didn't want commitment, until I got no commitment. I just felt it within me. I wanted more. I did want commitment to Levi, to my favorite gym, and yes, even to stickers. And I'm so thankful I had the chance to realize that.

The Love You Deserve

"Some think love can be measured by the amount of butterflies in their tummy. Others think love can be measured in bunches of flowers, or by using the words 'for ever.' But love can only truly be measured by actions. It can be a small thing, such as peeling an orange for a person you love because you know they don't like doing it." —Marian Keyes

I opened the door of my van, wearing lingerie, heels, and a long coat. Levi quickly walked through the airport terminal to get to me, clueless as to what was about to happen. Once he got to me, the van door slammed shut and fun was had. (Update: you know how I was talking about amazing sex before? We're at a whole new level these days. It just keeps getting better and I don't know if there's any better news I can give you than that.)

Levi and I had been in a relationship for less than two weeks. He flew from California to Austin, Texas so we could spend our first Valentine's Day together. He got us a beautiful Airbnb in the best part of town. He let me plan which restaurants I wanted to go to all weekend. He got me my first Chanel perfume set. He told me he loved me. It was magical. It still is magical. It keeps getting more and more magical, not just because he buys me things or takes me to fancy dinners, but because the man has an absolute heart of gold.

He has never once made me question how much he cares about me or how much he loves me. He makes me feel so secure that he's all-in on this relationship and wants me and me only forever. He gives me vitamins to take every morning and makes me sleepy time tea at night. He tells me how lucky he is to have me and why he loves me every night and makes himself tear up at the thought of it. (Sorry Levi, I just had to tell them...it's the actual sweetest thing ever.)

He has the hard conversations with me that I don't even want to have. He knows if I'm not fine when I say I am fine. He talks to me about his life purpose and biggest insecurities. He makes me feel more safe and protected than I've ever felt. He pushes me to be better. He believes in me. He wants what is best for me, always, even when I don't want it. He makes me think in new ways. He challenges me. He grows with me. He makes me the best protein shakes and yogurt bowls (and every other meal of the day to be honest.)

He just loves me so damn hard, harder than I've ever been loved. And I deserve that.

You deserve that, even when it feels impossible and even when your brain comes in with unsolicited advice and tells you that you can't have it all or that you should probably keep the mediocre partner you're with because what if you can't find better. Once you find it, you'll know. You'll feel more treasured than you ever have.

On the days when you can't fully love yourself, they'll be there loving you hard, harder than you could have loved yourself. You deserve that. You can have it all. Let your mind open up to the possibility that this could be possible for you. You deserve the partner of your dreams and all of the love, more love than you think you deserve.

Exercise: Allowing Love In

You deserve all of the love. Not because you've done anything to deserve it. Just because you exist.

1. List three things you love about yourself.

2. Visualize yourself in your ideal romantic relationship.

3. What do you want to believe about your lovability? Use the creating new beliefs exercise to practice your new thoughts about yourself.

4. Look for reasons throughout the day for why you deserve all of the love and how you're lovable. Write them all down.

Break the Pattern

"If you want something you've never had, you must be willing to do something you've never done." —Unknown

I really was not planning to fall in love with Levi. He wasn't planning on falling in love with me either. However, we both noticed something interesting about our relationship that changed everything.

We both broke our relationship patterns and tried something new with each other. I stopped going for "my type" of guy. I stopped escaping any romantic relationship with traveling. I stopped chasing men for the thrill of them falling in love with me.

A few years ago I flew to Austin, Texas to go on a date with someone who dumped me. Now I have Levi flying to Austin, Texas to spend Valentine's Day with me. Levi put far more effort into pursuing me than he previously had with other women. He kept trying instead of giving up that first time when I said no thanks. He was super vulnerable and let me really get to know him.

We both did the exact opposite of what we had always done and we created the most incredible relationship. Breaking out of the pattern of what you've always done can be really, really difficult. It's scary and unknown. It's uncomfortable. (But we are practicing getting really good at feeling the uncomfortable, yes?!)

It seems crazy and like it's definitely not going to work. But if what you've been doing isn't working, try something crazy. Do the opposite. Keep leaning into what feels uncomfortable because it's unlike what you've always done. See what happens.

Exercise: Try Something Different

1. Think of an area where you want to create different results. It could be relationships, the amount of money you make, your weight, your hobbies, etc.

2. Make a list of at least seven things you are currently doing in that area that are creating the results you have. They could be seemingly good or bad things.

3. Go back to that list and write down what it would look like to do the opposite of what you're doing now.

4. What stood out to you? What do you want to try in order to get different results?

5. Would you be willing to try the opposite, even if it didn't work at all, just to try it and see what happens?

Learn in Love

"Time has a wonderful way of showing us what really matters."
—Margaret Peters

I watch *The Bachelor*. Not just *The Bachelor*, but *The Bachelorette*, *Bachelor in Paradise*. All of them. Something I always notice on dating shows is that SO often, people use the reason "there's just no spark" to end a relationship. I used that reason before, too. I totally understood what they meant.

I had it all wrong. I can't tell you the number of dates I went on that were counted as failures because there wasn't that immediate spark or connection. Usually my date and I never wanted a second date because of the lack of sparks.

The "relationship master" in me knew that a relationship wouldn't work if one of us liked each other more than the other. I thought there needed to always be an equal and extreme love for the relationship to work out. As soon as I felt as if one of us had more feelings, I fully believed it was over.

I was waiting to fall in love, to be swept off my feet, to immediately want to rip his clothes off and have no doubts in my mind. I wanted to "just know" he was the one.

But I didn't. None of that happened. I had *lots* of doubts. The feelings didn't feel equal. I didn't feel the sparks. But Levi didn't give up on me. There was something in me that kept wanting to spend time with him.

Yes, he sure did take me on the best dates ever. Maybe that was it. Or maybe it's exactly what was supposed to happen. We both kept trying.

We learned a lot about each other. We were both vulnerable. I learned a lot about myself. And one night when he took me out to dinner, I realized this was something I never wanted to lose.

I didn't fall in love with Levi. I learned in love with him. And we still keep learning and growing. I have so much confidence in our relationship because it isn't something that just happened to us. We created it.

I don't think enough people talk about the importance of learning in love. When I say learn in love, I mean get to really know someone and fall in love with who they are on the inside, at their core, with the good and the bad parts, falling in love because you fully know them.

In movies, we usually see that immediate spark and then love happens. I think in life, this isn't usually the case. Love comes after vulnerability and intimacy (not necessarily sex, just closeness). That's why people who are friends first end up making such great lovers. Because they learned in love instead of expecting love at first sight.

You can't see all of someone at first sight. And all of someone is what we fall in love with.

Next time you're starting a new relationship, be willing to learn in love. Be willing to spend more time with that person before you decide you don't feel that immediate spark, no matter what kind of relationship it is. Get to know them, to really know them. Find out what makes them who they are. You might end up finding there is so much more love around you than you thought.

Shit and The Fan

"These pains you feel are messengers. Listen to them." —Rumi

Shit is going to hit the fan. Not just once. A lot of times. And it's supposed to.

It doesn't mean anything has gone wrong. Even though it's going to feel like that. It's going to feel really wrong. It's going to hurt your heart more than anything has hurt your heart before. But it's what's supposed to be happening.

Not having problems in a relationship would be like having someone build a successful 50+ year business that nothing ever went wrong with. It's impossible. Businesses keep going. A business keeps trying new things to find what works. A business learns from what didn't work and moves forward. It's the same with a relationship and the fights, pain, and upset don't mean you should stop trying and learning and growing. (Of course there is a point when you do need to stop and leave a relationship, but that's not what I'm referencing here). The fights should be things you are both learning from so you can improve and move forward.

I left Levi's to drive 20 minutes to my mom's house on a Thursday night at midnight. I cried most of the way home and then cried in my childhood bedroom. I couldn't stop scrolling through social media, not because I wanted to, but because of the pain I felt when I put my phone down and all of the thoughts about the fight we just had flooded in.

My heart hurt more than it ever had. My brain kept replaying the night, mostly the part when Levi was super sweet and tried his best to make everything better and made me feel so loved. But I still left anyway. It was a long night staring at my phone, hoping he would text me, even though I knew he was already asleep.

In the morning, we talked and resolved the issue. When one of us feels hurt, we typically hurt the other person and know how to do it well. That was a big thing we had to work on.

Levi has so many strengths in communicating and solving issues. He is always available to talk about the super uncomfortable shit I absolutely don't want to talk about. That's one of the many things that gives me so much confidence in our relationship: the fact that we're both willing to learn from what goes wrong and we actively try to do better each and every day.

We do the uncomfortable shit. Together. We learn from what happened. And we move forward. Shit is supposed to be hitting the fan. Is it moving you forward together?

At the time of writing this, we are almost nine months into our relationship. I have learned A LOT. We have had a lot of fights over nine months, too. Here are my best tips I can give for when shit hits the fan (or actually just anytime) in your relationship:

1. **Start couples therapy.** Seriously. It's never too early or too late to start and it's an absolute game changer.
2. **Go to therapy separately**. If there's anything I've learned being in a relationship, it's that I realized I have a lot more to improve on than I realized.
3. **Take time apart, even when you'd rather spend 24/7 together.** It's good for everyone.
4. **Learn what triggers the other person so you can understand them more and have more patience with them.** Trauma responses are going to happen and it's easier to have compassion when we understand why they're happening.
5. **Figure out what makes the other person upset.** You can call Levi all of the names in the book without much reaction, but if you call me silly at the wrong time, I might start sobbing(that's an exaggeration, but name calling is a sure way to make me upset).
6. **Use "I feel _____ when you _____" and "The story my mind is telling me is that _____".** When Levi tells me how he's feeling and is vulnerable in that way, we have a MUCH more productive conversation.

7. **Talk about your feelings instead of pretending everything is okay.** I'm still learning to be okay with crying and being emotional, so this one is a big work in progress for me.

8. **Don't just leave the situation when you're upset.** Talk through it and let it be uncomfortable. If you really do need space, let your partner know. Tell them you need space, but you're coming back to them in x amount of reasonable time and that you still love them.

9. **Practice saying no when you mean it.** If you really don't want to go to the bar while the guys play pool all night, say that. Don't say yes when you mean no. Compromise when necessary and do things you normally wouldn't for the benefit of the relationship as a whole, but don't keep saying yes to things you mean no to.

10. **Say sorry and be quick to realize your faults.** Own your end. Make it right. Have every intention to do better going forward.

Those are just a start. I've learned SO much and I continue to mess up and learn as I go. I'd love to share more details about our relationship and all that we've learned in another book one day. Levi has an incredible story and so much to offer. And together we have made SO much progress in our relationship. So here I am just putting that into the world. Levi, ready to write a book? ;)

Creating Your Own Extraordinary Relationship

"Instead of thinking how hard your journey is, think how great your story will be." —Andy Frisella.

Now that you've heard about my journey, I want you to be able to create an extraordinary relationship for yourself, too. These are the things that I've learned over many years of dating and relationships that have led to me being in a relationship that is better than I could have imagined.

1. **Do the things you love and be yourself.** You won't see it for a long time but everything you do and the person you are will bring you to exactly where you're supposed to be. If I hadn't been that weird girl who brought her dog to the wedding, I don't even know if Levi would have talked to me initially. If you're the girl who needs to bring her dog literally everywhere like me, be that girl, and be her shamelessly. Because I had just worked up the courage to leave my big-time job, I had a ton of extra time to get to know Levi and therefore fall in love with him. I could feel that good things would come from me leaving that job, and I was courageous enough to listen. Looking back, everything worked perfectly because I was showing up as me and following that inner, intuitive voice inside of me that was guiding me so I could end up exactly where I'm supposed to. Be who you are. You don't

need to hide all of the things that make you, you. Listen to those gut feelings, even when it's scary. And it'll all work out for you.

2. **Commit.** I was the kind of girl who wouldn't even commit to a gym membership or to sticking a sticker on something because those kinds of things are just not super simple to undo. So as you could imagine, committing to a relationship didn't come naturally to me, either. But what really helped me make this decision was I asked myself "What if either way turned out amazing?" If I was single and that was amazing, or if I was in a relationship and that was amazing, which one would I choose? The reality is that both options will be amazing sometimes and crappy sometimes. There's no perfect decision for anything. More than anything, we will determine if the option is amazing or not by the way we're thinking about it. So with that being said, if the commitment or decision turned out amazing, would you want it? It was a no-brainer hell yes for me.

3. **You deserve to be more loved than seems humanly possible.** Don't settle for anything less. Your person is coming and they are SO worth it. Remember that.

4. **If what you're doing now in your dating life isn't working, be willing to totally switch it up.** If you typically like chasing partners, try sitting back and not chasing at all. Or in my case, I was very set on not wanting to date or chase anyone at the moment at all so I could go do fun things alone. If you typically sit back and play hard to get, try chasing a potential partner and see what happens. Don't get stuck in the patterns of what you've always done. Switch it up. Try something new. And most of all, have so much fun whether you're single or in a relationship. That's the most attractive thing of all.

5. **Be willing to learn in love instead of fall in love.** I think so many people could really find love so much easier if they were willing to learn about the other person first before deciding to stop pursuing the relationship. Getting to that place where you can both share from the depths of your heart and be vulnerable will connect you on such a deep level. I ended things early on with Levi because I didn't feel that immediate spark and thought that meant something was wrong. It wasn't wrong at all. I just didn't know him deeply enough to see his flame. And the more I got to know him, the more he was vulnerable. The more I was vulnerable. We were both more vulnerable than was comfortable. It's scary, but it has brought us so close and has taken that spark and flamed it into a wildfire. Let yourself get super vulnerable, way more vulnerable than you want to. It will feel uncomfortable and scary, and it's supposed to. And you'll be able to create the deepest love.

6. **Know that shit is going to hit the fan and don't give up so quickly.** I can't tell you how many times the thought "It would be so much easier to be single" crossed my mind when we first started dating. Being in a relationship can be hard. There's a lot to learn. But we both had a conversation in the beginning and committed to each other, even when times get hard. But when those hard times come up, commit to learning from them. Look at them like an outside person observing the situation. How were you in the wrong? Do you like how you showed up? What do you want to do differently next time? Get therapy if you need it (but I think everyone needs it). It will be so helpful to get you through anything going wrong. AND with all of that being said, you still always have the option to leave the relationship. You

don't even need any kind of justification, you can just leave because you want to. I want my relationship to be a hell yes. If it's not a hell yes for me, it's a no. You get to decide that for you.

Chapter 5: Create Extraordinary Finances

"Women belong in all places where decisions are being made. It shouldn't be that women are the exception." —Ruth Bader Ginsburg

I'm not a financial advisor, but I love learning about money. There is an energy around money. Money is attracted to you or repelled by you. And the amount of money in your bank account is directly related to your mind. I still have so much to learn about money, but I've made an incredible amount of progress. Money can be fun. You can create more money than you dreamed of. More money in the hands of good people is always a good thing. You can make massive positive change with money. This is my experience so far with money and how to have more of it. It's uncomfortable work, but it's all worth it.

$40k to over $100k

"The only impossible journey is the one you never begin."
—Tony Robbins

I first typed this chapter title at the end of 2018 before I made this leap. I knew I wanted to write a book one day so I started documenting. When I read it now, I get chills. I made $40k that year. I wrote the chapter title as if the increase to $100k was guaranteed to happen. I had no idea that it would actually become a reality. I wanted to prove it was possible. And I did.

It wasn't an accident that I went from making $40k to $100k. I made it happen. Here's how.

I was laying in our bed in Melbourne, Australia, face down in the blankets on a Sunday afternoon sobbing. "I don't know. I don't know why I'm so upset, I just am." I didn't really know why I was so hysterical. But I felt bad that I was crying so damn much lately, almost daily to be more specific.

That morning, I went to a networking event held by Lululemon where we did yoga and goal setting. I had no friends in Melbourne; it was just me and Ryan and his friends. I didn't want to do things alone. But I committed to attending 20 events alone to go meet people, and this was one of them. So I packed my three meals for the morning that were all measured out because I was prepping for my bikini competition. I planned to take the bus but was late, so I hopped in an Uber which took me to the wrong address. After finding where I was going, I ran into the event late and stressed with my arms full. We did yoga and we set goals. I already knew exactly what my 2019 goal was going to be.

I wanted to make $100k in my business. I didn't care how, whether it was in my business, or working full-time. After we all wrote our main goal for 2019, they asked a few people to share. Being the kid who would have rather taken a Razor scooter to the ankle than to raise my hand, I knew that getting uncomfortable AF was how I was going to grow. So I raised my hand and said that I wanted to provide $100k of value in 2019. (Of course I spun my answer a little because making money seemed shameful and I wanted to seem like some kind of "good" human who didn't just care about money.) PS. I am now an amazing human (and always was) and I absolutely love money.

Once I said my goal to the group, the reaction was kind of like wowww ok. Or maybe that was just what it seemed like to me. I assumed they thought I was greedy and shallow. Maybe it was just me thinking my goal was greedy and shallow. It didn't feel good. After the event, I socialized a bit and handed out my business cards. I just felt all of the uncomfortable feelings.

Then I walked to a park to eat my meal— cold meal-prepped chicken. I ate alone and then headed to find the closest gym to get my big bikini competition workout of the day in. The gym that day was a struggle. I kept taking long breaks. I couldn't stop thinking. It took me hours to finish my plan and I still had to do cardio later. Everything felt so hard.

Once I finally finished, I took an Uber back to the apartment. Everyone was there hanging out—Ryan and his friends, and their friends. They were drinking and playing games. I got back gross, sweaty, and feeling like ass. I walked in pretty much with my head down to lock myself in the bedroom. And I still had to do cardio.

This is when the face down in bed, balling my eyes out came into play. "Why am I like this? Why do I have to want to do such big shit? Everyone else is just enjoying their life and drinking and playing video games and I just always want to do such hard shit. I just want to be normal."

Setting the huge goal gave me all of the feels, some feelings of excitement, but mostly terrible feelings. Every doubt in my mind showed up. Every insecurity was at the forefront of my mind. That's what happens when you set huge goals. Your mind goes crazy. Let it.

Set the huge, unrealistic, impossible goal. Then let your mind freak out. It's okay. It's uncomfortable, but it's okay. It's exactly what's supposed to be happening. This is why most people don't set huge goals. They don't want to feel the massive discomfort, the self-doubt, the 'who am I to achieve that kind of goal?'

It's easier to set smaller goals. We don't want to set the massive goal and fail. So we fail ahead of time. We don't even set the goal we truly want and decide to not even try.

I decided I didn't want that life. I didn't want the smaller, safe, realistic life. I wanted a 'holy shit' life. I wanted to create a life that set an example for other people out there who wanted that life too, but were too scared to go get it. I wanted to create a life that was a trailblazer for other people. I wanted to create a life they said was impossible.

If you're anything like me, I want to help you create that for yourself too. After I set my impossible, unrealistic goal of making $100k in a year, I wrote 100 huge actions I would have to take to accomplish that goal. I made a vision board. I chose a word of the year: willing. I had to be willing to do absolutely anything it took. I got coached on my mindset. And I got to work.

I'll share with you what I wrote down at the end of 2018 when my goal felt terrifying. I suggest you follow that same format about your impossible goal for the upcoming 12 months.

My 2019 impossible goal is to make $100,000 USD.

It will be accomplished by December 31, 2019.

The exact result that proves I achieved it will be $100,000 in all/any sources of income to my bank account.

My current thoughts on completing my goal are:
That's a crazy insane amount of money. I don't know what I have to do to get it. I feel like I need more time. I automatically think I should work more hours to make more money, but I know that's not true. I will need to be brave and make lots of offers. I will need to make sure my coaching is amazing. But I feel like I won't have time for anything else in life and I will need to work ALL the time. I just need to work smarter instead of more. I will need to be brave and make offers and invest and not be afraid to be turned down. I will need to make about 3x what I am making right now: $8,333 dollars a month. I guess when I think of it like that, it's not crazy, but it's still tripling my income!! So crazy.

The person with the traits necessary to accomplish the goal is:
- Organized with their time and someone who plans carefully (I need to make time each year, month, and week to plan my goal and what I am going to do to reach it)
- Extremely proud of what they do and secure in the knowledge that they're great at what they do

- Aware they can help (I need to believe I can coach and offer value)
- Not afraid to tell everyone who they are and what they do (this means reaching out, talking to people, making new friends)
- Brave
- Independent
- Able to focus on things that will improve themselves (stop doing things if I don't want to do them—stick to my calendar and put myself first)
- Always learning and growing (make clear monthly goals)
- Able to do thought work (do my coaching work daily)
- Careful and detail-oriented (I need to take more time and triple-check everything I do)
- Organized with systems (have a calendar and follow it)
- A planner who sets big goals (plan ahead of time and batch things)

This is how I will think once I am the person who has reached my goal:
- I am awesome and I can help so many people
- Making $100k per year is no big deal
- I have so much to offer
- People get so much value from what I provide
- I have systems and I'm not all over the place

This is how I will act once I am the person who reached my goal:
- I plan my weeks, months, and years
- I do things even when I don't feel like it
- I do self-coaching
- I stick to my calendar and priorities

- I am productive
- I take plenty of rest
- I am organized
- I put myself out there
- I help others
- I provide value

The person I need to become to achieve my goal has these characteristics and skills:

- Bravery
- Confidence
- Planned
- Consistency
- Follow-through
- Prioritized
- Detail-oriented
- Willing to volunteer
- Social
- Helpfulness

100 massive actions I will take to try to accomplish my goal (I crossed off the ones I actually achieved in that year):

1. ~~Start a podcast~~
2. Do a weekly Instagram or Facebook live with an offer for coaching
3. Post a blog weekly
4. Send a weekly email
5. Leave business cards at a new gym every week and talk to front desk
6. Meet somebody new each week, really get to know them, tell them about coaching
7. Take acquaintance out for coffee each week and tell them that I coach
8. Spend good quality time with a close friend or family member once a week and tell them about coaching

9. Meet someone new once a week and tell them about coaching
10. Invest at least 50% of the money I make from coaching back into the business
11. Keep a full list of expenses for the year
12. Plan the year
13. Plan each month
14. Plan each week
15. Stick to my plan no matter what
16. Message one person on Instagram each day and provide value to them
17. Spend 10 minutes engaging on Instagram six days a week
18. Take Sundays totally off social media, my phone, and work
19. Hold a workshop
20. Apply to work at three yoga studios
21. Make 10 variations of Facebook ads including ones with video
22. Post asking for feedback about Facebook ads, freebies, and website
23. Pitch myself to be on 10 podcasts
24. Ask for a raise at current job
25. Work for an online company teaching English
26. Get a job with [friend who owns company]
27. Attend and talk on three coaching program live calls every month
28. Run a webinar and advertise on FB ads
29. Work no more than 40 hours per week
30. Create a meetup group
31. Create a public Facebook group
32. Attend one other fitness meetup a month and make one good connection where I talk about coaching
33. Batch blogs, emails, and Instagram captions weekly
34. Invest in coaching for myself
35. Post in both Huntington Beach Facebook pages
36. Post on Criaiglist to coach in person
37. Find a real life mentor and meet with them once a month
38. Take a new class every week and meet one new person
39. Write six chapters of a book
40. Leave business cards at 20 coffee shops
41. Post on my personal Facebook once a week regarding coaching/transformation/what I'm learning
42. Schedule phone time/digital protocol
43. Set rewards for monthly achievements
44. Volunteer to coach for free for coaches/community

45. ~~Get 500 people on my email list~~
46. Hire a designer to make everything consistent/high class
47. Send a follow up email to everyone I've met
48. Invite all Facebook friends to like my Facebook page
49. Make a valuable video on story at least once per week
50. Make an offer once per week on Instagram
51. Post three times per week about 1st Phorm
52. Make three new Amazon Merch items every week
53. Advertise Amazon Merch with paid ads
54. Advertise Amazon Merch in Facebook groups
55. Do a giveaway on Instagram
56. Go to an in-person 1st Phorm event
57. Bring greens product I love to the gym
58. Send follow up message to all people who tried the greens
59. Create a system for engaging on Instagram and who to engage with
60. Send emails to five people a week from the gym
61. Work from 10 different coworking spaces and leave business cards
62. Follow up with people I met at coworking spaces weekly and make an offer for coaching
63. ~~Complete a big fitness goal and share the story on Instagram~~
64. Do a meetup twice per week
65. Speak at a live event and provide value
66. Create a money plan and know what I need to sell for the rest of 2019
67. Complete a more in-depth class on a business skill (marketing, blogging, SEO)
68. Finish all videos in Scholars
69. Complete all Entrepreneur and Money Worksheets
70. Make three new relationships
71. Hold 45 phone consults
72. ~~Ask my job for more coaching work~~
73. Dress like I make $100k DAILY
74. Do a big clean up — only keep the things that are beneficial
75. Join new Facebook groups and engage for 15 minutes daily where I provide value and add friends
76. Plan a retreat for 2020 and get seven women signed up
77. Attend Stacey's retreat
78. Get on a LCS coach's podcast
79. Publish a book
80. Teach yoga for lululemon

81. Create six 1st Phorm recipes to share on social media
82. Message 10 US people per recipe asking them to try it
83. Be enrolled in 100k or Master Coach programs
84. Speak at a JT Foxx event
85. Do a monthly what worked/didn't work list
86. Make one direct message or in-person coaching offer daily
87. Post weekly in Certified Coach community
88. Do all fails that worked well from first three quarters
89. Pitch to 10 magazines
90. Pitch to 10 popular bloggers
91. ~~Pitch to hold an event for Lululemon~~
92. Use all podcasts for Youtube
93. Send 10 personal emails per month to coaching people who said maybe later
94. Create systems as if I am someone who makes $500k
95. Enroll in Stacey's $200k Mastermind
96. Provide referral awesome gift
97. ~~Hire an assistant~~
98. Pitch 10 major blog sites — Forbes, etc.
99. Become a sponsored 1st Phorm athlete
100. Talk to one stranger per day and give them a business card

As you can see, I didn't even do the majority of my 100 actions. I didn't need to. Just doing the very few actions that I did take got me to over 100k.

It blew my freakin' mind. I thought it would be so much harder to make 100k than it was. I just kept trying. I didn't know how I was going to do it. I guessed. I made an all-over-the-place plan. I kept checking off things on my list. And I accomplished my goal.

Did I doubt myself? Of course. Did I feel like I knew what I was doing? Not at all. Was it hard? Absolutely. But it was much less of a big deal than I thought it would be.

I proved to myself I could do something that seemed absolutely impossible. I made over 100k when I had very little belief that I could. I learned that I really could do anything that I set my mind to. And that was the biggest prize of all.

Exercise: Impossible Goal Work

My impossible goal is:

It will be accomplished by:

The exact result that proves I achieved it will be:

My current thoughts on completing my goal are:

The person with the traits necessary to accomplish the goal is:

This is how I will think once I am the person who has reached my goal: (these should be written in present tense as if you already think these things)

This is how I will act once I am the person who reached my goal: (these should be written in present tense as if you already think these things)

The person I need to become to achieve my goal has these characteristics and skills:

In my coaching program, I have my students create 25 massive actions to take within the first 3 months. Brainstorm 25 actions you can take for the next three months that are MASSIVE. Remember, you may even fail at these actions as you attempt to achieve your impossible goal. That's how big they should be.

1.
2.
3.
4.
5.
6.
7.
8.
9.
10.
11.
12.
13.
14.
15.
16.
17.
18.
19.
20.
21.
22.
23.
24.
25.

Constraint & Consistency

"Do not try to do everything. Do one thing well." —Steve Jobs

Now that you have the secret to accomplishing all of the goals, you probably have 327 goals you'd like to accomplish. I do too. You probably want to accomplish them all right now, ASAP. Me too. But there's something important you need to understand.

Choose ONE big goal at a time. Practice constraint. Just one goal right now. Because otherwise you're going to choose 10 at the same time, and will burn yourself out and you'll end up with four successful days and 361 days of feeling bad that you're failing. Choose *one*.

But how do you choose just one? Choose the goal that you want most, that will have a wonderful overall impact on your entire life, or choose the goal that seems most fun and exciting. Typically there's one goal that will change so many other areas of your life. For example, my amazing Impossible Goal client and fellow coach, Breakup Coach Dorothy, chose the impossible goal of making $30k per month working 30 hour weeks. Because she reduced the hours she was working, this positively impacted her relationship, her social life, how she showed up as a business owner, and her feelings of readiness for motherhood. Choose the goal you want more than anything and will change everything.

You're also going to choose your goal, and then want to change it. Your mind will tell you to stop trying because it wants you to be efficient and conserve all the energy...AKA staying the same. Doing new things, especially when it gets super hard, goes against what your brain naturally wants to do. You have to stick with it. Be consistent. You've heard this one hundred times already, right? "Consistency is key." "The only way you will see results is if you're consistent." "Hard work without consistency will lead you nowhere." The world preaches consistency like it's required to do amazing things.

But as coach Kristen Carder will tell you: *inconsistency* is what will lead to success. The first time I saw in her email that the people who succeed are those who show up inconsistently, I almost sent her a message and told her there was a typo. That didn't make any sense to me. But the more I learned, the more it made perfect sense. You don't have to be perfect and consistent to get the results you want in your life. You just have to keep going. Be *persistent*. You're not going to be perfect. That's okay. That's normal. I try to work on writing this book an hour every single day. Sometimes I do spend an hour every day writing this book. Sometimes a week goes by and I haven't written at all. I'm not perfect. Or consistent. But I keep going. I know it's going to be done before the year is over for sure. That's the secret to sticking with your goal. It's okay to not be perfect or consistent. That's human. Just don't stop.

The first huge goal I chose was losing weight. That was the ultimate struggle I had always had and the one that I thought about the most. While I did want to lose weight, I also wanted to make more money, learn how to do a handstand, create a consistent morning routine, meditate daily, read more books, and stop feeling so damn busy all of the time. But I stuck with one goal and because I went all in and learned the skills necessary to get to a weight lower than I was when I was 16, all of the goals I completed after that were so much easier.

Weight loss skills helped me get a raise and make more money. Weight loss skills helped me with the mental aspects of running a marathon. Weight loss skills helped me manage my time because so many goals are made up of similar concepts: planning, failing, creating a new plan, feeling incredibly uncomfortable emotions, and not stopping until you reach the goal.

Because you're a human with a human brain, you're going to want all of the goals immediately. You think you won't be happy or have a better life until you achieve them all, but that just isn't true.

Choose one huge goal. Constrain yourself. Go all in on that one thing. Don't give up until you get there. Evolve as a human. Repeat.

And in case you're curious, here's a timeline of my accomplishments and impossible goals. The stories in this book aren't in chronological order, so here's what it looked like in real time.

2013 — Caught the travel bug after studying abroad at Cambridge in England.

2013-2018 — Went to college for Childhood Development and Human Services. Did a lot of babysitting. Budgeted a lot and spent all of the money I made on traveling. Traveled to about 20 countries, some alone and some with my friend, Kaitlyn. Learned about life coaching and "digital nomads" — people who travel and work remote.

2018 — Set my first impossible goal to weigh 125 pounds, which is less than what I weighed in high school. Lived in New Zealand for a year. Got my first "big girl" job doing remote Customer Support. Got certified as a Life Coach. Prepared for the bikini competition. Accomplished my impossible goal of reaching 125 pounds.

2019 — Set an impossible goal to make 100k in a year. Got my dream job. Kept traveling. Competed in a bikini competition. Ran 12 half marathons and 1 full marathon in 12 different states. Accomplished my impossible goal of making 100k.

2020 — Set an impossible goal to make 225k this year, but decided halfway through the year that I didn't want to keep hustling that hard and do things that made me happy instead. Bought a converted #vanlife van and my dog, Wilder, and traveled all over the United States in it. Met Levi. Did not accomplish my original goal, but felt great about my change in plans. Left my job at the end of the year.

2021 — Set an impossible goal to write a book. Started a relationship with Levi and started therapy, which both led to so much growth. Took six months off to travel in the van and to build our relationship. Stopped drinking alcohol. Accomplished my impossible goal of writing a book.

As you can see, I specifically chose just one goal for the year, but many other goals and accomplishments. I always do my best to keep my focus on my one main goal, but am open to other things I want to do *as long as they don't take away from my main goal.*

You'll also notice I didn't accomplish my impossible goal one year. I redecided during the year and changed course. Totally okay to do. Just make sure you like your reasons for doing so.

Happiness for Money and Approval

"Train yourself to let go of everything you fear to lose." —Yoda

"It sounds like you're trading your happiness for money and approval." That's what my coach, Krista St. Germain, told me on one of our calls. "Can you say that one more time?" I asked her. She did and it hit me. She was totally right.

I was making $150k and had six weeks paid time off. I got to fly first class to our quarterly meeting and stay at the Four Seasons right on Lady Bird Lake in Austin, Texas. I got to jet ski in the Cayman Islands on a Monday morning and got paid for it. I worked remotely and made my own hours. I got to learn from the best of the best.

But I knew it wasn't right for me. That's the only way I can explain it. In my heart, in my gut, in my inner knowing and in my intuition I wasn't feeling it. I was trying to convince myself that it was right.

Working for this company was my dream job. Other people would have killed to be in the position I was in. I was so lucky to have this job. So why didn't I want it? In my heart, I could feel that there was more for me. That although at one point, I thought this was the greatest thing in the world, I now knew it wasn't.

My intuition said let go. It'll all be okay. Moving on is the right choice for you. This is the beginning of something absolutely amazing. I knew it was the right move for me. It was right for the company. It was right for the position.

Making and having money is super fun. But I quickly realized money really wasn't what made me happy. I truly thought it would. I thought that when I was making $150k with six weeks paid time off, life would be great. People would respect me. I would be able to pay for other people to help me do things I didn't want to do. I believed I would be the most generous person. I thought I'd buy a latte from my favorite coffee shop on the beach and take a little beach walk before work every morning. I believed I'd wake up and be happy every day.

What really happened was that I started to feel pretty sad all of the time. I cried more than I used to. I noticed myself starting to live just for the weekends. I wanted to drink to escape more often. I wanted to eat ice cream to escape more often. I wanted to scroll Instagram to escape more often. I started being less and less happy with my life and more and more inclined to escape it.

I wanted the approval I got when I told someone I had a director level position or that I made over $100k at 26-years-old. I was trading my happiness for money and approval. I finally decided enough was enough.

I let it all go. I knew there was more. There was a better life out there for me. I could have both money and happiness. I could approve of myself if I had a high-level position or if I was unemployed. And I was right.

I let it all go. Because it was time to make space for even better things. It's easy to trade bad for good. But it's much harder to trade great for potentially amazing because uncertainty is a difficult thing to grapple with.

Exercise: The Crisis Checklist
Whether you're 25 or 45, use this quarter-life, mid-life, anytime-in-life crisis checklist to help you get through what you're going through. It will help you get clear and make a decision based on what's best for you, not just emotional decision-making.

1. What's the crisis?

2. Are you feeling emotional as you think about this? If so, plan a time in the future to work on this. Actually schedule it in your calendar. If not, keep going.

3. What are all of your fears around the decision?

4. Are you convincing yourself logically one way or another? If you remove your mind's fears and all of the convincing you may be doing, what does your inner knowing (the one that knows it WILL be okay) say?

5. What do you think my advice would be to you right now?

6. If you believed in yourself 100%, what would you do?

7. If your 80-year-old self were to give you advice right now, what would they tell you?

Responsible Investments

"Don't be careful. You could hurt yourself." —Byron Katie

I was telling my coach that I felt bad spending large amounts of money on things I wanted just for me, things like my van, my dog, and things that make me feel pretty. I felt irresponsible, like maybe I would look back and regret spending that money if I needed it for an emergency in the future.

When I was working full-time, I was saving 50% of each paycheck and putting it straight into savings. But I still felt like I might be spending the other 50% irresponsibly.

My coach had me question what was responsible spending. What does that even mean?

I told her that putting all of my money into investments was really the only super responsible thing I could do with my money, because it felt safe and responsible. She reminded me that there are many people who believe just the opposite. There are people who have been burned by putting too much money into investments and now believe that's an irresponsible way to use money.

Some people think buying cars is the best way to use their money. Other people think college is the most important. Self-care. Makeup. Shoes. Plastic surgery. Travel. Coaching. Online courses. Dogs. Donations. The stock market. Investment properties. The opinions are endless.

Almost everyone has a different opinion about the best way to spend money. We pretty much just make it up, and then decide if we want to think about it in a positive way or not. People can lose tons of money in the stock market and still decide it was a great decision because at least they tried. Other people can spend money on clothes and shoes and feel like that was the best way to spend it.

There is not one correct way to use and invest our money. It's absolutely worth researching, but ultimately you get to decide what responsible spending looks like for you. It depends on how valuable that thing you're buying is for you.

I was stressed about making a $12,000 purchase. My coach asked if I was offered a new $12,000 Tesla, would I be stressed about purchasing it? No, I wouldn't because I believed that a Tesla was worth so much more than that. It would be worth every penny to buy it at that price.

Is what you're investing in totally worth the value? If not, change what you're investing in or truly look at all of the value you're getting from it.

I learned that sometimes it's irresponsible for me to save. I miss out on so many life experiences I would have had otherwise when I'm just focused on savings. I miss out on yummy lattes with friends or trips I never took.

Sometimes responsible investing to me is spending. What does it look like for you?

Looking at many things that I feel like are super responsible through a "what if it were actually irresponsible" lens is one of my favorite things to do.

One of my incredible clients in my Impossible Goal Coaching program had an impossible goal to get back to what she loved to do most, painting, and make money from it. Here's what she shared in our community after a coaching session we had about how her hustling to make money in other ways than painting was actually irresponsible: *"You just helped me so much!! Thank you. Instead of feeling like I'm irresponsible for painting — I totally see that it's irresponsible NOT to be filling myself up with what I love, grounds me, connects me to people for all the right reasons, and allows me to move my body, and stoke my inner child. I'm going to go journal NOW to capture this mental shift while it's fresh. Thank you!"*

Exercise: Responsible Spending

1. What is your favorite splurge item ever? Why was it worth it?

2. Notice, it was worth it because you THOUGHT it was worth it. Not everyone would agree with you. But you believed it was a great splurge because of all of your thoughts about it.

3. How much money do you want to save and invest? How much do you want to spend?

4. How can you set up your lifestyle so that's possible? (I seriously lived in a van for a year so I could save money!!)

5. What is the item you want to splurge on?

6. How is it not responsible to buy this? Let your brain get it all out.

7. But how IS it responsible to buy this? How is it the most responsible choice to do the thing that brings you joy?

Look at both options. It might be more responsible than you think.

Becoming Rich

"Having money isn't everything, not having it is." —Kanye West

When I first went through coaching and thought about my relationship with money, I didn't understand why keeping my "I'll never have enough money" attitude wasn't helpful. I got coached time and time again until it clicked. This is what I finally learned.

1. **People who think they don't have enough money live in a space of deficiency.** This doesn't feel wonderful. Believing I didn't have enough money always kept me in a place of wanting more, being unsatisfied, and a little bummed out. If you focus on not having enough, you will always feel a little desperate and completely unsatisfied.

2. **People who think they don't have enough money will always think they don't have enough money.** It's wild. A person who has $15 and believes they don't have enough will likely still feel that way when they have $15 million. The amount of money in the bank is not what determines what you think and feel. You do. No matter how much money you have, your beliefs and feeling of insatiability will not change until your mind does.

3. **People who think they don't have enough money create not enough money.** It took me a while to understand how I could believe I had more than enough money without actually making a shit ton of money. If I believed I had plenty, how would I not be motivated to go get more? But you will be. When I thought I didn't have enough money, I kept doing things that didn't get me much money at all. I accepted a life of little income. I kept babysitting and working at a preschool and doing work-exchange programs.

It was only once I started to believe I was rich that I actually started to create it. I believed I deserved more. I believed money I spent would always come back to me. I increased my income by ten times. I toyed with the idea that it wasn't an evil thing to have money. I considered it could be true that I was rich and I was open to receiving more. No, not in the private jet, designer handbag way. But in the way that I am an American living in California with the privilege to be able to have low living expenses so I can travel and still make money from my laptop. Compared to the rest of the world, most of us truly are wealthy.

I am rich. I had never let myself believe that before. I am rich. I believe being rich is amazing. I believe more money should be in the hands of good people who came from nothing. I believe more money should belong to women and minorities. I believe it's okay to want to be rich, even when the world says otherwise. I made a list of all of the things I would do if I truly believed I was rich and I started living as if I were rich. I told myself that when I was rich, I would get eyelash extensions. So I got them, and soon changed my mind that they weren't worth the hype and decided my natural lashes were pretty, too. I decided that when I was rich, I would donate monthly to my best friend's third grade classroom, so I did. I send flowers to someone I love every single month. I plan to hire a diverse group of women to help me in my business. I decided that when I was rich, I would get massages every week. So I found a place that let me buy massages in bulk: $250 for 10 massages. I started getting massages every week and tipping well. I told myself that when I was rich, I would work in beautiful places that I enjoyed. So I got a membership to the spa at the Hyatt Huntington Beach. It was $115 per month, but I got a $100 credit to use at the spa each month to use on a service like a massage or facial. (Yes, apparently there is such a thing as a spa membership and I was all in.) I got discounts at the restaurants in the hotel the spa was at so I could have coffee in the morning from a cafe, work, and have an ocean view in the background. I could also use the hotel pool and jacuzzi, so when I was answering emails, I could do it from the jacuzzi. I could use all of the spa facilities, so I would sit in the zen spa waiting room with a selection of snacks and drinks and get my work done there. When I was there, I acted more confident, I presented as professional, I was happier, and I probably even did better work because I was in a gorgeous environment and felt better.

It was while I was sitting outside one afternoon at the Hyatt working when my manager asked me to hop on a Zoom call. We hardly ever met on Zoom. I was a little worried. When my video turned on, she could see the reflection of the palm trees on the glass windows behind me. She offered me a promotion—a huge promotion, from part-time customer support rep to the full-time Director of Customer Support. This was the job I had been trying to get for two years. $125k salary. Six weeks paid time off. Amazing health benefits.

I was rich! It was true. Being rich is a state of mind. You get to decide if you're rich or not. I couldn't find a downside to having that belief. I felt classy, I showed up well, I got shit done. No, I didn't blow all of my money. I manage my money like a badass. I spend my money on investments and things that bring me joy. I spend my money on people and causes I care about deeply. And on things that will help me get closer to becoming the person I want to be and to achieving the dream life I want to have. That's it.

I buy fewer clothes that are better made and will last years and years, and rent clothes monthly so I don't end up buying things I'll only wear a few times. I make much fewer impulse purchases. I make more purchases that will help me get closer to becoming the person that I want to be. Believing you're rich does not mean you will immediately go spend all of your money. Rich people spend their money extremely carefully and extremely well. Once that clicked for me, I was all in. I believed I was rich, and a lot more money came to me.

Money isn't everything. We know that. Especially at this point in time when this book is being written (2021) when it kinda feels like the world is falling apart. And while there are plenty more important things in life than money, many of us have a strong desire to make more money. Not all humans have that same desire, so if you have it, follow it. Keep in mind what could be possible. Find inspiration in others who are doing what you want to be doing. Make money and become rich for good. For yourself. For your family. For the world.

Exercise: What Makes You Rich

1. If you had the exact life you wanted and money wasn't an issue, what would it look like? What are all of the things you would do differently?

2. What little way can you start showing up as that version of you now?

3. How would that change how you show up in the world?

4. What blocks do you have to believing you are already rich?

5. What negative things do you think would happen to you if you believed and acted as if you were rich already?

6. Are those things necessarily true?

7. How could believing you are rich now make you into a BETTER person? Into more of the person you want to be?

Having More Than Enough

"Shine a great light on your most amazing qualities. We tend to focus on the negative aspects of us and forget all the greatness that we have within." —Harnaam Kaur

I have more than enough money. I'm still working on believing that. It doesn't feel completely true yet. I write that along with nine other thoughts I'm working on believing in my journal every morning. Sometimes I can get behind the belief that I'm rich, and other times I still freak out about not having enough money. My brain comes up with all of the reasons that "I have more than enough money" is not true when I think about it. But the more I practice thinking it, the more my brain starts to find little pieces of evidence that it might be true.

I do have more than enough money to survive. I do have more than enough money to live the way I'm living. I do have more than enough money to live a good life that I enjoy. I do have more than enough to buy what I want at the store. And I even have more than enough money to buy flowers for someone I love every month.

Having more than enough money can feel like it's a bad, dirty thing. We tend to think that people who have more than enough shouldn't have that much because they should be using their money to help other people or make the world a better place. Even just writing down that I'm working on having more than enough money makes me feel a little funky, like it's a bad thing. But let's think about it.

What if Oprah decided she didn't want more than enough money? She has donated tens of millions of dollars. Without having more than enough, she couldn't have donated that to others. Most people, even if they are just donating 10% of what they make, believe they have more than enough and therefore can help others.

Believing we have more than enough creates generosity. It's what I believe when I donate to my best friend's classroom fund. It's what I believe when I buy another friend a coffee. When I fully believe I have more than enough, I show up as more of the person I want to be.

If I believe I have more than enough, won't I just get to a place where I give everything away and end up without the wealth I want? Nope. It's quite the opposite. The more that we believe we have more than enough, the more we feel able to accept money and the more we are willing to ask for more money because we are confident that our work is worthy of massive compensation, and that money will be safe with us and put to good use. Believing you have more than enough will keep creating more than enough for both you and the people around you. On the surface, it seems crazy, I know. I thought so, too. But I think I could be right about this one.

Believing you have more than enough will change the way you feel and show up in the world. It will attract more money to you. You will feel safe having, keeping, and sharing money. You do have more than enough. You just have to be willing to believe it.

Exercise: Abundance

1. What is one thing you want more of right now? Is it more free time? More friends? More love? More success? More peace?

2. What have you tried already to get more of that thing?

3. What is your fear in believing that you already have enough of that thing?

4. Are you willing to try believing you already have enough to see what happens?

5. How is it true that you have enough of it now?

6. What's the worst case scenario?

7. Remember you can always go back to the way things were.

8. Make a list of 10 new beliefs you want to believe about having enough. Write them every day. Practice thinking them. Plan time daily to write them. Your brain will almost never automatically think them at first, so you have to think them on purpose.

9. Notice how you feel when you think these new thoughts. Do you feel good? Excited? Optimistic? That's how you know it's working. The way you feel is super important.

Investing

"It's funny how day by day nothing changes. But when you look back, everything is different." —C.S. Lewis

It was final. I signed the paperwork, but honestly I wasn't quite sure what I had just signed. I was 25-years-old and was still in my travel-the-world phase. This was when I was getting paid well, and before I left my job and did #vanlife with my dog. I just purchased a house. Alone. I had a mortgage and a hell of a lot of responsibility. I felt both proud and scared.

I bought it as an investment, not a house I wanted to settle down and live in. I learned from my grandpa at a very young age that if you invested right, you could be set up for a successful future. He owned a few houses that he rented out for income and traded stocks. I saw that he wasn't struggling like other people in my life and I knew I wanted to learn from him. He was living the lifestyle I wanted.

While it's completely f*cked up that it's infinitely easier for people who already have money to make more money off of their money, I believe there are also little things most everyone can do to take steps toward a more financially secure future.

I am extremely privileged that I am white, grew up with financially educated people I could learn from, and had a secure family to help me so I could save the money I was working for. I was also very willing to sleep on floors (even an airport bathroom floor to be specific), strangers' couches, and eat peanut butter and jelly sandwiches for weeks on end. I made sacrifices to save as much money as possible and learned how to save hardcore.

I trusted my grandpa's advice and decided to buy a house in Las Vegas. I got a big-time job and kept my expenses extremely low. I wanted to invest now to create my ideal future.

Invest as much as you can as soon as you can.

Here's an example of realistically what could happen based on a study by *Business Insider* that kind of blows my mind.

A 25-year-old starts saving $300 per month in a savings account with about 5% interest.

A 35-year-old starts saving $300 per month in a savings account with about 5% interest.

A 40-year-old starts saving $600 per month to make up for lost time in a savings account with about 5% interest.

Here's what happens:

The 25-year-old **saves $144,000** into their account and, after all the compound interest takes effect, will have a **balance of about $460,000** when they're ready to retire at 65.

The 35-year-old **saves $108,000** into their account and, after all the compound interest takes effect, will have a **balance of about $251,000** when they're ready to retire at 65.

The 40-year-old saves the most amount of money, **$180,000** into their account and, after all the compound interest takes effect, will have a **balance of about $359,000** when they're ready to retire at 65, which is about$ 100k less than the 25-year-old.

As soon as I learned about this, I set up a transfer of money automatically monthly into a savings account.

The moral of the story is that the sooner you start, the more your money will make money. Money in a savings account will actually decrease in value over time. The amount will stay the same, but inflation will happen and the same amount of money will get you less over time. If you start putting money into a savings/investment account in your 20s, you'll have more money when you retire than if you started at 40 and put double that amount in savings.

No amount of money is too small to start saving. Take the money out first, as soon as you get paid and put it away into another account so it's like you never got it. You can even get it deducted directly from your pay so you never actually see the money. Start that habit of saving. You will *always* feel like you can't save no matter how much you're making. You can save a little. Practice that skill, and it'll pay off. Saving $1 a week now will help you save $100 a week later because you've already gone through the discomfort of giving something up and are in the habit of automatically saving.

Investing can look totally different — it can simply be adding a small amount of money to an investment account monthly, learning about stocks, or as big as buying a freakin' house. I just highly recommend you do it. Do your research. Eat PB&Js when you need to. Treat yourself with a nice oat milk latte when you need to. And spend and save on purpose.

Exercise: Save Now

1. Start by tracking your expenses. Do it weekly or monthly, because if it gets to be more than that, it can get super overwhelming. I have a spreadsheet I create each month with all of my expenses and what they are for. This helps me make sure I don't have any incorrect payments and that there are no subscriptions I may have forgotten about. Without awareness there is no choice. Start with becoming aware of how much you're spending and on what.

2. Decide what you want your goals to be. Do you want to reduce spending? Do you want to contribute a certain amount to savings monthly? Do you want to just start with learning where the heck to start investing long term? Decide on your first goal and work on that.

3. Before you are about to buy something or send through that Amazon order, ask yourself "what if I didn't need to buy this?" It can seem like a silly question, but my mind surprisingly finds reasons I actually don't need to buy the thing and great ideas for

what to do instead. Try this and list three times it worked. What did you do instead of buying the new thing?

My Most Unique $40

"We should all start to live before we get too old." —Marilyn Monroe

There are a lot of ways to make money. People make ridiculous amounts of money on TikTok and Youtube. They post a protein bar and make thousands of dollars. The possibilities are endless. Not just for them, but for you, too.

Man, was I excited. I even told my mom the news. I had to tell someone. It seemed kinda crazy, but also fun. I had thought about making money this way for a while.

A few years ago I even asked my mom what she thought and I was so surprised that she told me to go for it. I always thought about crazy and fun ways to make money that were also easy. So this day was a pretty exciting one.

I had just sold a pair of my used panties online. For $40. Yes, I did.

It felt like a super easy, kind of ridiculous, absolutely random, and just slightly scandalous way to make a few extra bucks.

It felt fun to make money doing something that felt in no way like a job.

Give yourself permission to do what ya gotta do. Have fun on the way. Question why society tells us to do or not do things. Get out of your comfort zone. And sell a pair of panties online if you want to just because it seems kinda fun.

When I was 17, I used to be a background actor and made pretty dang good money doing it. I was mostly on the Nickelodeon show, Victorious (with Ariana Grande). But was also in a couple of other things including an Audi Superbowl commercial. It was such a fun, random job that I wouldn't have even imagined until I met a friend who was doing it.

Try whatever you're drawn to because it's possible to make money in all kinds of ways. Step out of your comfort zone, whether it's posting more vulnerable things on social media, posting your art for sale on Etsy, or selling some undies. See what happens. The possibilities are endless.

Exercise: Anything is Possible
1. Write five ideas of how to make money that seem crazy but also that intrigue you. Keep this list for when you're ready to try something new.

Chapter 6: Create an Extraordinary Daily Life

"You are not a drop in the ocean. You are the entire ocean in a drop."
—Rumi

I believe your dream life is created by living your dream days over and over. It starts with making each day amazing. Once you can love each day of your life, then your life becomes extraordinary.

How to Live Your Purpose

"Western cultures believe we must be alive for a purpose - to work, to make money. Some indigenous cultures believe we're alive just as nature is alive: to be here, to be beautiful & strange. We don't need to achieve anything to be valid in our humanness." —Lanie (Twitter @melatoninlau)

It was the first conversation in which I felt like Levi and I really bonded. We were sitting outside for dinner at a fancy steakhouse. It was the kind of restaurant you go to celebrate something special. It was like a little taste of what my dream future would feel like. We ordered incredible appetizers that I ate so much of, I could barely eat any of my meal. Of course I finished the dessert, though. Priorities.

Levi was telling me during dinner that he felt like he wasn't really living his purpose. But to me, it was clear as day. He was living his purpose so hard. He couldn't see it. He had been completely sober for a year and a half. He was the only person at the parties we would go to who didn't drink, yet he was always the life of the party. He lost 100 pounds and always was the hype man at the gym encouraging people to keep going. He was in therapy and had completely changed the person he was into someone many looked up to. He inspired people. He got messages from people all the time telling him that he inspired them.

He was living his purpose loud and clear. But he didn't feel like it. I couldn't help but think of when I didn't know my purpose either.

For as long as I could remember, I felt like I needed to do more. No matter if it was in college, working and going to school full-time, or when I had a challenging full-time job. As each day ended, it seemed like I still had a todo list that never ended. I couldn't rest and sit down and watch tv because of the restlessness I felt. I always felt like I just didn't get enough done, but I was so busy no matter what. I measured my worth based on the amount of things I got done. I doubted myself and if I was enough. But what often happened was I felt so overwhelmed, I would spend time distracting myself from feeling overwhelmed by having a snack, looking at my phone, or even doing things that weren't my priority just to have something to do and feel like I was being productive. No matter what, I just always felt bad. I knew I wanted to do things differently. I wanted to feel better. I wanted to find this mysterious purpose of mine that was in a dusty corner somewhere so that I could actually feel good about my life. I didn't know what my purpose was, but I was pretty sure I hadn't found it. I for sure would have been a better human and I'd feel much better when I started living my purpose. But...How do you find your purpose? How would I even know when I found it? Was my purpose pre-written or did I get to create it?

And then in life coaching, I heard this:

You are already enough and completely complete. You don't have to be better, give more, or save the planet. Your purpose is humanness. You are done. You are complete. You are already purposeful. You are already magnificent. Your reason for existing is to exist. That is your purpose. You don't have to do anything to fulfill your purpose in life. Your life is your purpose

What, what? I don't have to find my purpose because I'm already living it? That seems crazy. But I considered it. My mind had been telling me for so long that I needed to do more and be better that I just thought it was 100% true.

I considered that maybe what my mind was telling me wasn't true. Maybe I was already purposeful. My purpose could be right in front of me. Maybe I was *already* living my purpose. I couldn't stop thinking about how things would change if I believed I was living my purpose already right then. What would be different if tomorrow, all day, I believed that I was living my purpose?

If you don't believe you are living your purpose, you will never feel like you've actually lived your purpose. Someone with zero accomplishments and someone with 1,000 amazing accomplishments can both feel no sense of purpose. It's not because of what they're doing in the world, it's because of the way they're thinking. No matter what you accomplish, you could always feel like you have no purpose if you don't let yourself believe you actually have one and that you're living it.

It seems like if we accept we don't need to do anything differently to live our purpose that we would just never work and eat cookies all day. But the opposite is true. Once we accept that we are already whole and enough and there is nothing we have to do on this earth, we get to choose a purpose that we want to do. It gets to be fun and exciting. We don't *need* the cookies and unemployment because we feel good and live a purpose we love. We do more from a place of feeling good. We get curious and try all kinds of things that fill us up.

I finally started to believe it just to see what would happen. My purpose on this earth was exactly what I was already doing and what I wanted it to be in the future. I was truly doing exactly what I was supposed to be doing. But here's the catch, the more I truly believed that, the more I lived into my purpose. The more I stopped beating myself up for not being better, the more I could feel better in my own skin and give back. The more I could show up as the person I wanted to be. The more I lived out the life I wanted to live.

At the gym, I started to be a little more intentional and encouraging, believing that my purpose today was to go help my teammates achieve their goals. At work, I started to take more time to connect with the people I was around and be kinder when the inevitable little things would bug me. When I talk to my family after work, I started being a little more present and showing a little more love. I tried to go bigger in my business to help more people. I give more because I already feel grateful and whole.

I knew that the little things I was doing were helping me live my purpose and I was doing exactly what I was supposed to be doing in life. By trusting that I wasn't off track and that I was in fact already living my purpose, I put more care and intention into each day. I became more and more of the person who I wanted to be. I knew that even when things went wrong, I was learning from them and getting better.

I was living the life I was supposed to be living. Nothing had gone wrong. It was all going according to plan, even when it didn't feel like it.

In the past few weeks, I've been doing a lot of sitting on the couch, eating mac and cheese, and watching *90 Day Fiancé* (AKA what I'm literally doing right now as I write this chapter). How is that my purpose?"

Your overall life purpose is not defined by a period of your life. This period of my life involves a lot of *90 Day Fiancé*, food that tastes amazing, spending literally 24/7 with Levi, and slowly writing this book.

I could truly create a convincing argument that I'm not living my purpose right now. I'm making almost $150k less than I made last year. I went from waking up at 4:30am, getting a killer workout in, and getting things done all day to sleeping in until 8:30am and just kinda chillin' all day. I've gained more weight than I planned on within the last two years. I travel less than I used to. I don't yet have a wildly successful online business with a huge following of people who I'm helping change their lives. I don't volunteer anymore. I'm taking this year to write my book and build a relationship.

I could make a damn good argument about how I'm not living my purpose. But you know what that would do? Keep me powerless. Keep me stuck. Make me feel like shit. And send me into a shame corner where I'd get further from the person who I want to be.

Even if you don't feel like you're living your purpose yet, consider that you just might be doing what you need to today. Your purpose today might be just as important as your future purpose. Your steps to get to the person who you want to be are just as vital. And if you don't know who you want to be in the future yet, trust that you're finding it.

You're getting closer every day. Keep chasing after what you desire. Ask yourself what sounds like something fun to do today. Your purpose today is getting you closer to your future purpose. You're living it. See what changes.

Exercise: How to Live Your Purpose

1. What kinds of things are you excited and passionate about?

2. What brings you the most joy?

3. What is fun to you? What things make you lose track of the time?

4. What did you used to love that you've stopped doing as you've gotten older and busier?

5. If you believed you were already whole and enough, what amazing things would you want to do in the world just because you wanted to?

6. What things feel embarrassing or scary to do, but you know deep down your soul wants to do them?

7. How are you going to make the world a better place?

8. How do you want to be remembered?

9. How could it be true that you are already living your purpose today in some way?

10. Practice believing all day one day that you're living your purpose. Set reminders for yourself so that thought keeps coming up. Just be willing to really believe for one full day that everything that's happening is part of your purpose. At the end of that day, come back here and reflect on the day. What were you thinking? How did you feel? Did you show up differently?

Creating Habits

"Success is the product of daily habits—not once-in-a-lifetime transformations." —James Clear

Habits are something that really intrigue me. I think habits are such an important part of our lives and what we accomplish. But we don't focus on them enough. We focus on the BIG things. We focus on impossible goals and hustling. We need to focus on those small things that we do every single day. In the moment, they seem like they don't matter much. What's another snooze button hit, mini Dairy Queen Blizzard (one of my favorite desserts ever), or skipping working on your goal for today to go spend time with friends? It doesn't seem like it matters much in the moment, but those little things compound every single time to create bigger results.

I really wish I could tell you that I've become the master of habits and ALWAYS do what I plan to do. I wish I could tell you that each and every day after I wake up easily at 5 a.m. ready to take on the day, I meditate for 10 minutes, do tapping, visualize, read 10 pages, stretch, workout hard for an hour, journal, walk 10k steps, close the rings on my watch, moisturize, never eat sugar, make a list of my top five priorities, and call my mom. I wish I could tell you that my life is perfect and I have the key to creating all 700 habits you'd like to create in the day. But I'm not and I don't. The truth is I've tried to create tons of habits all at once to add into my day and it just has never worked for me.

I have created some pretty cool habits though by doing one thing at a time. I close the rings on my Apple watch everyday except for when I'm sick or traveling or on the rare Sunday. I read 10 pages of a personal development book before bed about 50-75% of the time. Before bed every day no matter what, I tell Levi why I love him that day, ask him about the best and worst part of his day and tell him mine, we pray, and we say three things we're grateful, two things we're grateful for but don't have yet, and one thing we want to improve on personally.

Some habits are easy to create, and others are harder. For me, habits are so much easier when I have accountability. The habits that Levi and I create together are so much easier for me because on days when I just want to go to bed, he is there to make sure I still get our evening routine done. He will know if I don't do it. He's there to help me. I also have accountability in my coaching groups. We are all there to hold each other accountable and check in often to let everyone know how we're doing and get support when we need it.

If you want to learn more about creating habits, James Clear is your man. His formula to create a habit is:
1. Make it obvious
2. Make it attractive
3. Make it easy
4. Make it satisfying

I've created my habits following that formula:
1. My evening routine is obvious because Levi will remind me if I forget. We do it at the same time of day so bedtime is always a reminder that it's time for the routine. We also have a book sitting out so we see it and it's there to remind us to read.
2. It's attractive because we've compiled it with things that we chose and that make us both feel good.
3. It's easy because it's short and simple.
4. It's satisfying because we love being told why we're so loved and being grateful out loud feels amazing.

Another reason why my evening routine habits have stuck so well is because of habit stacking. This is also something I learned from James Clear. Habit stacking is adding a new habit to something you already always do. So, an example is after you brush your teeth, you add a new habit. Since you always already brush your teeth, it will help you remember to add your new habit. We added our evening routine habit in right after we got into bed. So we get into bed, and we immediately do our routine. It's easy to remember because we get into bed every night already and it reminds us that it's time for the routine.

The final thing I've found that helps me create new habits is to add ONE thing at a time. Our evening routine started out with just one of those tasks. First, we just told each other why we loved each other. Once we did that perfectly and never skipped a night, only then did we add praying. Then later we added the best/worst parts of our day. And finally we added three things we're grateful for, two things we're grateful for and don't have, and one thing we want to improve on. This was over a six-month period. It was s l o w. We weren't in a rush to add 50 things to our evening routine. We added more once we were super confident with our current habits and wanted to add more. Do one thing at a time. Perfect it. Be patient. More is not better. And as always, practice the way you are talking to yourself in the process.

Exercise: Creating Habits

1. What are all 50 (or insert any crazy, unrealistic, large number) habits you'd like to have in your life if you could just wave a wand and have all of the habits?

2. Now pick one. Don't think too hard. Go with your immediate answer. Pick one habit you want to start (or stop) first:

3. How can you create accountability for yourself? (Friends, partner, a coaching group, etc.)

4. How can you make it obvious?

5. How can you make it attractive?

6. How can you make it easy?

7. How can you make it satisfying?

8. What are you going to habit stack your new habit with?

9. How will you know when you're ready to add a new habit in, once you have this one down?

More Happy and Less Hustle

"Once she stopped rushing through life, she was amazed how much more life she had time for." —Unknown

"What's your side hustle?" "You need to hustle to make it." Hustling is a thing that we glorify. People act like you'll only make it if you hustle. I've done it. I made a lot of progress towards my goals by hustling. And then I reached the goal...and didn't feel any better. So then what?

Let's go back to when I was 15-years-old. I got fired from my first job at a little snack bar on the beach because I wanted too much time off over the summer. When I was 19, some of my coworkers at Domino's pizza would get annoyed that I would take SO much time off. As soon as I started working, I chose jobs based on how flexible they were to me. This is something that was always important to me. I always knew that I wanted my life to be more important than my job. (I found out that you shouldn't directly say that to your employer though, especially when it's a nannying job.) I knew that when I was 80-years-old, I was going to be much more excited about the times I spent actually living than the times I was working.

Fast forward 10 years. Money became more important. The acceptance that came with having a career and my own health insurance seemed more valuable. I was working at least 40 hours per week. Along with work, it was important to me to go to the gym every day, and by the time I drove there, worked out, and drove home, it was about a two-hour ordeal. I had also recently gotten the cutest puppy ever that needed way more attention than I expected. I wanted to eat healthy and have time to actually make food instead of just picking something up. I wanted to be able to spend time with friends, read, enjoy the sunshine on a nice day, and play with my puppy. But soon I started to notice I was slipping into habits I didn't want. I was spending more time on my phone so I could turn my mind off. I started looking forward to the weekend more because I wasn't enjoying the weekdays anymore. Drinking seemed much more appealing than it ever had. I was looking for distractions because my life got waaay less fun.

I was working a lot (this is totally relative but it felt like a lot to me). I was thinking about work when I wasn't working. I always felt like I could never get done the things I wanted to get done. I didn't know how it was possible for people to have a full-time job, any social life, go to the gym, eat healthy and get enough sleep. Plus what would happen when I wanted to have a baby?! I could barely handle a puppy. The only reasonable thing I can think of is that moms get super powers because otherwise I'm completely stumped.

I knew something needed to change in order to keep my happiness and to create the life I wanted and knew had to be possible. So I started dreaming. If truly anything were possible, what would I want? What have other people done that I could figure out? What would the dream schedule be like?

I decided that I wanted to take a break from working to just get back to enjoying life, and then after a few months, work 20 hours a week. I thought my constant need to be doing something productive would be nagging me to get a job and work again. But the opposite was true. I was able to take six months off, travel in my van, and I enjoyed it way more than I thought was possible. I was able to slow down, take more walks outside, sit down and watch a movie, or heck, even binge watch lame reality tv allll day for literally the first time in my life without beating myself up for not doing something "better." And I was happier. I was living. I was doing more of what I wanted to do and less of what I felt I "should" be doing. (But honestly this break was possible because I spent years hustling and was lucky enough to be able to save some of the money I had been making during my hustle days.)

I realized I wanted more happy and less hustle in my life. And that DIDN'T have to mean I couldn't make as much money. Some of my favorite people in my life take a ton of time off, work a few days a week, and make lotssss of money. They are my example of what's possible. I'm not where I want to be yet, but I believe hustling isn't what's going to get me there. I believe what I'm doing in the 20 hours per week that I'm working is more important than how many hours I work. I believe I do much better work when I'm happy and have time to do the things I love. I believe I can provide a ton of value to the world without spending a ton of time doing it.

I want you to also have more happy in your life by practicing loving yourself. Love yourself without the attachment of what you've accomplished or how you showed up that day. Yes, you are amazing, but you are also SO loveable even on the days when you don't feel amazing at all.

This past Tuesday, Levi and I got invited last minute to a birthday party at a hotel cabana. It's the nicest hotel around and I had never been. So I changed my work schedule and spent the day at the pool celebrating our friend and making new friends. It was the most fun, spontaneous day. I was so thankful I had created a life where that was possible. My life is more important than my job, and I'm thankful I love myself enough to truly believe that. I have more happy and less hustle. I love myself regardless. And that's the best.

Exercise: How to Create More Happy and Less Hustle

1. How is it true that working less could actually benefit you and help you reach your goals?

2. What is one thing that is a priority in your life that feels like you don't really have time for, but you want to make time for?

3. If you knew you could reach your career goals and make the amount of money you wanted to make, how many hours per week would you realistically want to work?

4. List some ideas of opportunities that could make that possible. Do you own your own business? Do you work as a contractor and provide a ton of value to a couple businesses?

5. What brings you joy? How can you add more joy into your daily life?

Time Management (For Your Advantage)

"Eat a live frog first thing in the morning and nothing worse will happen to you the rest of the day." —Mark Twain

If you're anything like me, time management is hard. I've even had someone say I might have ADHD. While I don't think I have ADHD, I do have a cell phone that is designed to be addicting, a watch designed to be addicting, a puppy that is needy as heck, a computer browser that alerts me every time I get an email or work message, and a human brain that goes from thinking about work to what I need at the grocery store to the fact that my boyfriend should probably cut his nails.

I get distracted if I'm not doing something that gets me close to a flow state. And of course I get distracted, because we live in a world that is always trying to get our attention.

Over the years, I've tried lots of time management strategies. Overall, whichever strategy you are trying, please don't use it against yourself. Do not use time management strategies to try and do 500 things in one day. (Hi, I'm also talking to myself because my natural inclination is to squeeze as much in a day as possible.) Plan your free time first. Plan time with your loved ones first. Plan time to treat yourself first. Time management is not a punishment, so please my love, do not use it as one. Enjoy your life first.

Did you know, if we live a pretty long life, that we only have 4,000 weeks? Our whole life consists of about 4,000 weeks, and none of them are promised!!! That feels so small to me. The weeks go by so fast. 4,000 weeks is all we have. Make them count. Do fun things. Plan them on purpose. And ENJOY them.

Here are my favorite time management strategies. Use them for your advantage.

1. Power List — by Andy Frisella

The power list is a great tool I've used many times. It is writing down the five most important tasks you need to do that day. It is not a long-term goal sheet. It is a list of the most important five tasks you need to fully complete that day. If you've done those five priorities, you will have won the day. You will be moving forward in life.

2. Eat That Frog — by Brian Tracy

Do the task you're most likely to avoid and that will have the biggest positive impact on your life FIRST. Writing this book is my impossible goal for the year, so I make it a point to do it first. Also, writing this book is the thing that I'm most resistant to doing all day because it's difficult and vulnerable and honestly, I am so critical of myself and what I write. If I don't write first, it usually won't get done. Eat that frog. Do the hard, important thing first.

3. Monday Hour One — by Brooke Castillo, Lauren Cash, and Tyson Bradley

Monday Hour One is the main time management strategy I use, but it can also incorporate the first two I shared about above. The first step is to make a list of absolutely everything you need to do. This includes going to the grocery store this week, and also hanging up the

Christmas decorations in three months. List anything that pops into your mind when you think of things that need to be done. This will take a while, and you might need to go back to it a few times to make sure you've written absolutely everything down.

Next, you add all of those things to your calendar. Whether it's a paper planner or online, you give every single one of those things to do a spot on your calendar. This way, you can stop the recurring thought "Ah! I need to do _____ before _____." Write it all down and you won't have to stress about it every time you remember. Once it's on your calendar, it's as good as done. Make this list every week at the beginning of the week with any new things that have come up.

Now, it's time to plan for the week ahead. You have a bunch of things on your calendar, but when are you going to do them? Schedule the hours. Commit to the time you're going to do the thing. From 7-8 I write. 8:30-10:30 I'm at the gym. 11-11:30 I bring my car to get it fixed. 12-4 I work. 5-6 I coach. That's what my calendar looks like for one day. Notice that I leave some space in between for things like getting ready for the day, meals, and free time. Do not pack your day totally full. You'll have to estimate how long things are going to take, so just take your best guess and you'll start learning how long everything you do actually takes and become more accurate at scheduling as you go.

This method helps me incorporate the Power List and Eat That Frog, too. I plan my day in a way that the most important thing is done first, and I make sure all of my priorities are done. Sometimes I have a separate power list of the important tasks I want to get done like: follow my meal plan, read 10 pages, etc. If they're things I wouldn't necessarily include a time for on my calendar, I occasionally make a separate list.

Now here's the hard part: Actually following through on the things you say you're going to do! This is such a hard thing and one of my favorite accomplishments. I *never* used to be able to do what I said I was going to do, so I love having this skill now. First, be careful what you commit to doing. Do not create an unrealistic plan for yourself because it will create unnecessary failure. And once you have your plan, get ready for discomfort. You will want to do literally anything besides the important thing you are planning. Checking Instagram, walking the dog, and even cleaning the toilet will sound better. Recognize that, and do the hard thing anyway. We can do hard things.

And finally, my favorite part of time management and productivity is to turn your damn notifications off. Turn them off on your phone, your watch, and your computer. You truly don't need to be notified every time someone views your Linkedin profile. Keep them to an absolute minimum. The only notifications I have are for text messages (and all group texts are muted). Turn the red bubble notifications off, too. It feels so clean and will leave you feeling so much better, with plenty of mental space for getting sh*t done.

Here's a screenshot of my phone homescreen. It has my vision board as my background, and no apps. They're all hidden. I love how clean it feels. There are definitely no red bubbles because 99% of my notifications are off.

Exercise: Time Management

1. Try each of the three time management strategies separately, and then together.

2. Reflect on how it went. How did you feel?

3. Did any issues come up?

4. How can you improve for next time?

Stop Waiting

"The bad news is time flies. The good news is you're the pilot."
—Michael Altshuler

I stepped quickly across the slippery rocks. Barefoot, I could feel every jagged edge. The cold rain was pouring over every inch of my body. I had stripped down to my bathing suit. But I could feel the warmth of the margarita I enjoyed as I watched the sunset inside of me. I kept looking back to see if one of my friends would follow me. I had a feeling they would. I kept stepping and kept looking. I saw them watching me for a while, and then I got so far away I couldn't see them anymore. I was surprised they weren't coming. This wasn't even my idea.

It was a weeknight. I'm not even sure which day it was because I took the week off work. I was in Mexico, and every day was a party. There were five of us. Kyle and Issac, a new friend whom I had just met that day, and Kaitlyn — my best friend and forever travel buddy who I was trying to convince to quit her job and travel the world with me.

We headed to the beach in Tulum, Mexico. We were lucky enough to find the only free parking spot. It was for customers only so we had to get a drink and the little hut next to it. While everyone sat at the hut bar waiting for a round of margaritas, I laid in the hammock off to the side and dreamt about the life I truly wanted but was terrified to drop everything to create.

The beach was absolutely gorgeous, the kind of beach that looks like a screensaver. It took my breath away. But way too soon, big dark clouds were rolling in and we had to head for cover fast.

"Let's go for a swim in the rain." I don't even know who said it, but I quickly replied "YES. I'm in. Let's go." I live for that kind of stuff. An adventure with new friends and playing in the rain.

"¡Fondo, Fondo, Fondo!" I chanted to try to get them to chug the rest of their margaritas. They finally finished their drinks. I got up to go swimming, assuming everyone would follow. Whoever had the idea in the first place backed out. "Come on!! Let's do it! It'll be fun!" I said to try to convince at least one of them to come with me.

But nope, no one was coming. I considered not going. No one else wanted to go. I shouldn't go alone. It wouldn't be as fun without my friends. But something in me said go. Do it anyway. Stop waiting for everyone else and do what you want to do. So I stripped down to my bathing suit, threw everything I had with me in a pile under the table, and walked across the rocks to the beach.

I kept looking back, waiting for at least one of them to come, but they weren't coming. I had to tell myself to be extra careful because I was alone and it was getting really dark really fast.

But I wanted to go. I wanted to prove to both myself and them that I didn't need anyone to come with me. I wouldn't back down just because I would have to go alone.

As soon as I made it to the water, the world around me stopped. The cold rain was dripping down my face. The ocean water was so warm, almost like an endless jacuzzi. The color of the ocean was so light blue, it seemed unreal. The sound of the rain and the waves together was the most beautiful sound. I took a deep breath and relaxed into the magic of it.

It was exactly what I needed. It was perfect. And it reminded me...

I created this moment for myself. I could create whatever I wanted. I could do it alone. I didn't need anyone. I didn't need to wait. I didn't need to do it another time. I didn't need to convince anyone.

I could do it. Even though it was kind of scary. I hesitated. I questioned myself. But I did it anyway.

Maybe it's even more magical when I just have me. I have my own back. I trust myself. And I don't wait for anyone to want exactly what I want. I've got me. And that's the most magical thing there is.

Conclusion

That's how I've achieved the extraordinary goals I've always wanted. I went from being a $15 per hour making, food-obsessed, body-hating, uninspired girl to the woman I am now. I am SO incredibly proud of where I'm at, living (in a house, not a van) with the most incredible partner even though I grew up with no healthy relationships to learn from, with a job I love and a savings account and a house, and the cutest dog in the world (that's a fact), living as a woman who is a whole lot better at saying sorry and owning where I can improve, that has run 13 half marathons and one full marathon in 12 states, and has traveled to somewhere around 27 countries, and has lived out of a van and road-tripped the US, and has completely stopped drinking despide the patterns of addiction in my family, who has made $100k in a year when I had no reason to believe that was possible for myself, and has learned to take time to rest and believe I'm worthy for just who I am and not what I accomplish, but who also just loves accomplishing huge goals for the sake of accomplishing huge goals and evolving as a human to see what I can learn along the way. That wasn't a run-on sentence, was it? Maybe it was but hey, I ALSO just finished writing an entire freaking book and I can have a run-on sentence if I want one.

I'm living my impossible life. And I know there is a whole lot more coming. I've done a lot for myself in the first quarter of my life and I'm excited to do a lot more for others and the world around me in the next few quarters of my life. I needed to put myself first, and I think that's such an important place to be. If that's the stage you're in, no shame in that game at all. Don't feel bad about taking care of you.

Once I learned these tools, I had a deep desire to share them because they changed my life so incredibly much. I hope they have that same impact for you. Go create your impossible life. Achieve the extraordinary goals you've always wanted. That's your purpose. Keep following them. And please, keep me updated. I know you're going to create absolutely incredible things.

xx, Felicia Anna Broccolo

Thank you for taking the time to read this book. I put so much into it and I hope you got so much out of it. Make sure to visit **createtheimpossiblelife.com/justforyou** to get all of the exercises from the book in one place.

Make sure to get on my email list there to find out about all of the opportunities to get coached by me, or join my Impossible Goal groups. We have a community of women who also have big things planned and are all getting together to make it happen. It's my favorite place to be and I hope to see YOU there too.